YOUTH LEADER GUIDE

Loveland, Colorado

www.friendshipfirst.com

Group resources actually work!

This Group resource helps you focus on **"The 1 Thing™"**—a life-changing relationship with Jesus Christ. "The 1 Thing" incorporates our **R.E.A.L.** approach to ministry. It reinforces a growing relationship with Jesus, encourages long-term learning, and results in life transformation, because it's:

Relational
Learner-to-learner interaction enhances learning and builds Christian friendships.

Experiential
What learners experience through discussion and action sticks with them up to 9 times longer than what they simply hear or read.

Applicable
The aim of Christian education is to equip learners to be both hearers and doers of God's Word.

Learner-based
Learners understand and retain more when the learning process takes into consideration how they learn best.

Friendship First™: The 1 Thing You Can't Live Without
Youth Leader Guide

Copyright © 2005 Group Publishing, Inc.

Visit our Web site: **www.friendshipfirst.com**

Credits
Creative Development Editors: Kate S. Holburn and Beth Robinson
Senior Editor: Karl Leuthauser
Chief Creative Officer: Joani Schultz
"Mixed Messages?" Authors: Steve Argue and Dave Livermore
Copy Editor: Alison Imbriaco
Art Director: Jean Bruns
Designer: Sheila J. Hentges
Cover Art Director and Designer: Jeff A. Storm
Print Production Artists: Jan Fonda and Sheila J. Hentges
Photographer: Rodney Stewart
Illustrators: Kara Fellows and Sheila J. Hentges
Production Manager: Peggy Naylor

ISBN 0-7644-2894-2

10 9 8 7 6 5 4 3 2 1   07 06 05

Printed in the United States of America.

Contents

Welcome to Friendship First™!

You're about to embark on an adventure.

The teenagers who join you will never be the same.

Neither will you.

Friendship First makes a real difference in people who experience its life-transforming messages. These experiences affect the way they live. Your group's time together will move teenagers from just knowing about each other and Jesus to having a friendship with one another and God. These highly relational and experiential Get-Togethers promise to move youth from head knowledge to heart-transforming friendships. As your teenagers build friendships with one another, they'll find that Jesus is the best friend of all!

■ What is Friendship First?

It's a flexible, friendly, engaging 13-week series for small-group interaction that compares our friendships with others to our friendship with Jesus.

The purpose is to

- meet new friends in a fun, friendly, nonthreatening way;
- learn how friendships form;
- practice friendship skills; and
- discover and grow a friendship with Jesus.

■ Who's Friendship First For?

- **Anyone who desires great relationships!**
- **Youth of any age.** We've designed these Friendship First Get-Togethers to work for ages 12 through 18.

Check out **www.friendshipfirst.com,** which is your source for Friendship First information! Get more insight into the heart behind Friendship First, and find out about the Children's Ministry Kit, Adult Ministry Kit, and Church-Wide Kit. Use this Web site to order more leader guides, student books, CDs, and more!

- **People at any relational setting.** These Get-Togethers work for girls' groups, guys' groups, youth-group leaders, friends, classmates, interest groups, sports teams, co-workers, Bible study groups, new attender groups, and any existing group!

- **People at any spiritual level.** Those who have no faith in God, those who have expressed curiosity in spirituality, those who have believed since childhood but have put faith on the sideline, and those who have had longtime involvement in church will all find that Friendship First levels the playing field. It works because each tested experience is very purposeful.

■ Where can I use Friendship First?

Friendship First works within your existing youth ministry program.

It's great for Bible study and Sunday school, flexible for large-group/small-group formats, and easy for small groups!

No matter what your format is, be sure you (and other leaders) build relationships with youth and get involved. Participate in the activities, Daily Challenges™, and discussions. Friends come in all shapes, sizes, and ages!

> **Strengthen families!**
> Friendship First Get-Togethers even work with parents and their teenagers—together! If you value building strong friendships and communication skills in families, give it a whirl with combined ages.

■ How can I use Friendship First?

Because you'll form small groups of six to eight people, you can do Friendship First with hundreds, even thousands, of teenagers. There's one rule: Limit each small group of friends to no more than eight people. You may be tempted to fudge on this and expand your group to 10 or 12. Don't. A group of six to eight guarantees a positive experience and maximum participation by everyone. In this case, smaller is better.

Everyone is vital. When a group gets bigger, it's too easy for someone to "disappear." Talkers dominate; shy ones recede. Every teenager is important to this experience. Each friend has something to give. Each has something to gain. Remember, even Jesus limited his circle of friends to 12—and his closer circle to only three. If Jesus limited his scope of intimate friends, we can too.

It's possible to do the experiences with fewer than six, though. Jesus did promise us, "For where two or three gather together as my followers, I am there among them" (Matthew 18:20).

■ What do I need?

You'll need this guide, one *Friendship First*™ book for each teenager, one *Friendship First*™: *Youth CD*, and the supplies listed in each Get-Together. If you have more than one small group of six to eight, you might want to give each group leader a *Friendship First*™: *Youth Leader Guide* and let groups move through the Get-Together at their own pace.

Or you might choose to have one person facilitating from the front. Just form the multiple smaller groups, and give each of the small-group leaders a *Friendship First: Youth Leader Guide* (more available at www.friendshipfirst.com). The person at the front, who is leading the entire large group, can guide everyone through the activities together and then direct each small group to do the next appropriate section or discussion together. For example, if your church's youth ministry wants to begin each Get-Together with the High Impact meal option for everyone, do that. Have everyone eat together. Then lead the Get-Togethers, explaining each activity upfront, while everyone experiences the Get-Together in a small table group.

You'll choose the setting and leadership approach that works best for your situation. *One secret: Never attempt to do the activities as a large group.* Everyone needs to get involved on a one-on-one basis.

INSIDE SCOOP Our upfront leader was masterful at watching multiple groups. We found that some groups are just slower, while others are faster. Being the leader requires being comfortable with that fact.

We're offering lots of great Friendship First items that will enhance your small-group time and help everyone "take home"—in a tangible way—what you've experienced together. Scattered throughout the following pages, you'll see tips on including and using these fun enhancements!

Call 1-800-447-1070, 1-888-476-8755 in Canada, or go to www.friendshipfirst.com.

1 Thing lapel pin

Friendship First book

Friendship First greeting cards

Roofus the Moose plush toy

■ What happens at Friendship First?

STORIES AND SCRIPTURE

Everybody loves stories. So we've embedded all sorts of approaches to "stories" each week. Here's what youth will do:

- **Explore God's stories**—The Bible, which is jampacked with stories of God's friends, is the foundation for Friendship First. Scripture shows us what it's like to live for God. Plus, God reveals the best story of all—and we star in it!

"God showed how much he loved us by sending his one and only Son into the world so that we might have eternal life through him. This is real love—not that we loved God, but that he loved us and sent his Son as a sacrifice to take away our sins.

"Dear friends, since God loved us that much, we surely ought to love each other. No one has ever seen God. But if we love each other, God lives in us, and his love is brought to full expression in us" (1 John 4:9-12).

- **Tell personal stories**—God's story didn't stop 2,000 years ago. It's still underway. And each of us plays a starring role. Each week teenagers tell portions of their life stories so they can learn from one another and real life. Be prepared for open-ended questions that ignite great discussion and storytelling. No musty fill-in-the-blanks here.

- **Use the *Friendship First* book**—Each person gets his or her own copy of the *Friendship First* book, which explores friendship and gives examples of how to practice what he or she is learning. It's used in each Get-Together as a workbook and journal. Each week you'll encourage everyone to read a chapter of the book to prepare for the next Get-Together.

- **Watch DVD vignettes and interact with songs on the CD**—These multimedia treats evoke emotion and spark discussion.

- **Create shared experiences to make discoveries on the spot**—Each Get-Together makes fun, thought-provoking memories just by happening. Every creative activity provides immediate shared experiences to talk about, so groups create their own "stories." The activities are not gimmicks or throwaways. The shared experiences are strategically designed to help teenagers personally discover and learn more. You'll be leading experiential object lessons no one will forget.

FOOD AND FRIENDSHIP

Eating together is a hallmark of Friendship First. Who doesn't agree that food and friends go together? "Let's do lunch…let's go out for dinner…let's meet for breakfast…let's have coffee." Alan Loy McGinnis says in his book *The Friendship Factor*, "There is something almost sacramental about breaking bread with another and it is almost impossible to have dinner with an enemy and remain enemies."

Not only does coming together for a meal or snack break down barriers; the meal is itself a great reminder of our dependence on God.

Eating and meeting hold meaning. The food ideas take Jesus' words seriously. He gave his friends a lasting reminder of himself as he shared a loaf of bread and a cup of wine, saying, "Do this to remember me." (1 Corinthians 11:23-25). The daily requirement of food and drink reminds us of our daily need for Jesus. Plus, early Christian friends set an example for us: "They worshiped together at the Temple each day, met in homes for the Lord's Supper, and shared their meals with great joy and generosity—all the while praising God and enjoying the goodwill of all the people. And each day the Lord added to their fellowship those who were being saved" (Acts 2:46-47).

Each food idea adds to the "layering" of the Friendship First experience. The suggestions serve several purposes:

- to enjoy a relaxed time to talk,
- to create a memory-maker that ties to the specific Get-Together's theme,
- to involve others in contributing to the group, and
- to add fun and surprise.

We've given you choices with the flexible food options. Each food idea holds special meaning for the Get-Together. But you can choose from three different menu options depending on your time, setting, and energy level.

Quick and Easy — This menu option is for the no-prep crowd. It requires few utensils and one quick stop to shop. It's a simple way to make a point.

Easy Plus — OK, if you want to make eating a bit more memorable and fun, choose this menu option. Just a few extra touches will enhance the whole experience.

High Impact — This meal choice assures a Wow! It's our recommended option because it shows teenagers how special they are to the group and guarantees surprises. But you don't have to pull this off alone. Ask the party people in your group to help pull together these exciting themed meals. You'll be amazed at who wants to help!

DISCOVERY THROUGH DISCUSSION

Friends like to talk with each other. And you'll guide discussions with questions that encourage even the most reticent to speak up. Here's what you will do:

Talk about what just happened. Each Get-Together provides purposeful experiences to talk about and learn from. Think about it. When have you learned most? Has it been from a speech or sermon? a book you read? or something that happened to you? If you're like over 90 percent of the population, you learn and remember most from what *happens* to you. And what makes an experience even more powerful? Talking about it. Many of the experiences in Friendship First are experiential metaphors. By using the questions provided, you'll help teenagers discover for themselves special truths about their friendships with others and with God. So don't be tempted to skip the experiences or the questions that follow them!

Encourage one another. Every time you meet, people in your group will affirm one another. In a world packed with put-downs and "you're never good enough," Friendship First is an oasis in a desert. Each time they meet, your teenagers will practice being friends to one another by sharing sincere compliments. It's one more way to practice living our faith. "Don't use foul or abusive language. Let everything you say be good and helpful, so that your words will be an encouragement to those who hear them" (Ephesians 4:29).

Discover that Jesus is our friend. As an umbrella principle, the entire Friendship First uses the metaphor of human friendship for our friendship with God. Every time you meet, teenagers will understand more and more about Jesus' love for us as friends. You'll discuss and dig into that profound truth. You'll wrestle with how it could be and how we live it out through our relationships. God has put us together with people to demonstrate his love. "If someone says, 'I love God,' but hates a Christian brother or sister, that person is a liar; for if we don't love people we can see, how can we love God, whom we cannot see?"(1 John 4:20). And Jesus said, "I no longer call you servants, because a master doesn't confide in his servants. Now you are my friends" (John 15:15).

Do detective work. Everyone in your group will be given an assignment. Teenagers must watch for why they think God brought your group together. We believe that each small group that comes together will be God-planned and have a purpose: "For we are God's masterpiece. He has created us anew in Christ Jesus, so that we can do the good things he planned for us long ago" (Ephesians 2:10).

So what are those good things? As teenagers look for God's big plans for them and their friends, they'll talk about what God's plans are. They'll wonder why God put them all together at this point in time.

Join your teenagers in watching for what God is doing. Be sleuths together, and pray that God guides your discoveries. You'll all be surprised to find out just what God has in store.

Pray together. Every time your group connects, you'll take time to communicate with God. Sometimes

you'll talk to God. Sometimes you'll listen. The ideas are nonthreatening ways to pray so that anyone at any level in a spiritual journey can feel comfortable. You'll help teenagers discover that they can communicate with Jesus just like they communicate with a good friend.

FRIENDSHIP PRACTICE

Here's the practical, fun part. People won't just *hear* about ways to become better friends with one another and Jesus; they'll get chances to *practice*. Does it seem odd that we practice almost everything else in life? Lessons in school. Music lessons. Sports. Foreign languages. Driving. Dancing. You get the picture.

So why don't we practice living Christian principles?

Practice. Whenever you meet, you'll offer practical, real-life suggestions to help teenagers practice the concept you're focusing on. For example, when teenagers talk about tips for making friends, they'll stop and do those tips—try them on for size. Or when they're discovering the power of kind words, teenagers will actually say kind words to one another. Everyone will "test drive" giving and receiving kind words to see how it feels. Practicing during time together will help make God's ideas tangible and practical—and easier to try out when away from the Get-Togethers!

Commit to Daily Challenges™. Not only will teenagers apply biblical truths while they're together, but they'll pledge to practice between Get-Togethers as well. By committing to a Daily Challenge each week, teenagers will put God's friendship principles to work in real life—with their friends, family members, co-workers, classmates, neighbors, and strangers. Each Daily Challenge will lead to a fun experiment, which will be shared in the group as everyone reports what happened out in the "real world." You'll be thrilled to learn how your group is lighting up a dark world! "Let your good deeds shine out for all to see, so that everyone will praise your heavenly Father" (Matthew 5:16).

Teenagers will find the Daily Challenges in their *Friendship First* books. Join in the adventure and participate in the Daily Challenges, too!

■ What do I need to be a Friendship First leader?

Be you. That's right. The best leaders are the ones who are comfortable with themselves and willing to be real, vulnerable, and authentic. You're the best you for the job!

Then remember that it's not about you. It's about letting God work through you. "So we are Christ's ambassadors; God is

INSIDE SCOOP Let teenagers be the leaders. During our field test, multiple teenagers and adults shared the leadership load. Because Friendship First is so easy to lead, group members signed up to lead the week of their choice—and each one did an awesome job!

Use Friendship First to help peer leaders grow and learn leadership skills. And be there to cheer them on!

What makes Friendship First easy to use?

"Between Friends" boxes offer helpful tips and suggestions.

Between Friends

"Inside Scoop" boxes give hints, ideas, and insights based on our own field test.

 This icon lets you know it's time to share in pairs.

 This icon indicates that the questions are for group discussion.

 This icon highlights the "Jesus Connect" in the Get-Together.

 This icon alerts you to allow a specific amount of time for part of the Get-Together.

The Get-Together at a Glance chart provides a clear overview of the experiences and lists any supplies you'll need.

Get-Together at a Glance

---

making his appeal through us"(2 Corinthians 5:20a). God has put you with specific people in this specific time and place to represent Christ to them. Incredible! That's how God works!

Be warm and hospitable. Friendship First demands relational leaders. You know the old saying, "To have a friend, you must be a friend." These Get-Togethers revolve around friendships. If you don't feel comfortable reaching out to others, join a group, but don't lead one.

Be open. Be willing to honestly share your own life stories. Being transparent doesn't mean you have to "disrobe"! Honest disclosure involves appropriateness. You can tell about past struggles without giving details that make everyone else uncomfortable.

Be vulnerable. There's no need to be the answer person. In fact, it's permissible—and desirable—that you admit you don't have all the answers. Be willing to say, "I don't know."

Be willing to share the load. Find a co-leader, a friend, who can partner with you to lead portions of the Get-Togethers. For example, the eating times work best if preparation is handed off to someone who can concentrate on the food. Or designate someone to be the host to greet people on arrival. By sharing leadership, you're also modeling working together as friends.

Friendship First really works! That's because each Get-Together has been tested by real teenagers. Yes, real teenagers from the real world have already experienced this. We've made the mistakes so you don't have to! To make it even easier, we've added insider tips as "Between Friends," to be your helpful friends along the way. Through three decades of ministry together, we've seen the results Friendship First experiences produce. We've seen God work through friends, family, and churches in miraculous ways.

So, if you're wondering why you would use this published program when you know your group best, remember,

- **Friendship First is a step-by-step, carefully formatted plan.** We've provided a highly experiential series. Unlike the typical church programs that expect people to soak up information, believe it, and figure out how to integrate it into their lives. Friendship First starts with this premise:

| EXPERIENCES *lead to* | ┈┈▶ | BELIEFS *lead to* ┈┈ |

For example, which is more likely to happen when someone visits your youth ministry for the first time?

This?

THE EXPERIENCE:
People welcome the visitor with a smile, making him or her feel important.

THE BELIEF:
"Wow! People are so friendly here!"

Or this?

THE EXPERIENCE:
People ignore the visitor, making him or her feel like an outsider.

THE BELIEF:
"Ouch! People are really not friendly here!"

ACTIONS	*lead to*	RESULTS
		(life change)

THE ACTION:

THE RESULT:
Attending group/church

THE ACTION:

THE RESULT:
Not attending group/church

Our prayer is life change—youth exploring the depths of God's friendship and love with others. Therefore, we want to do what we've found to be most effective in bringing that about. Here's what happens in the process of Friendship First:

LIVING THE FRIENDSHIP FIRST EXPERIENCE:

People build friendships with one another in a fun, exciting, nonthreatening atmosphere that points to our friendship with Jesus.

"I have always seen myself as a 'friend-ly' person, but I realize there is more to being a 'friend.' Thinking about my best friend helps me see how I can grow closer in my relationship with Jesus. And having the chance to get to know a group of people with whom I had mostly only been 'friend-ly' helps give me the chance to work on being a friend! Not only has this helped me to grow friendships, but I have also grown closer to my husband, and I feel a closer, more personal connection to my Friend, Jesus!" —Deb

THE BELIEF:

People have fun getting together with friends and exploring how God is like a friend.

"After finishing Friendship First, we found it was just the beginning, because our group continued to meet and grow closer together! It's a life-changing experience, and it's the first thing I'm going to implement as the college ministry leader at my church." —David

THE ACTION:

"If this is what Christians are like, maybe this God stuff is all right too."

"Friendship First challenged me to reach out to others through experiences, tears, joys, and laughter. It's helped me to build friendships that will last a lifetime and has strengthened the most important friendship of all—my friendship with Jesus!"—Rebekah

THE RESULT:

People willing to go deeper and live out friendships with others and Jesus.

"I enjoyed every week of our Friendship First experience...food, fellowship, and fun proved to be a great combination for our group. I can't look at a meal without finding the similarity between food, faith, and friendships. I highly recommend this material to small group leaders who want to build lasting friendships." —Dave

- **Friendship First provides a highly relational experience.** We all live in a world of relationships. That's how we're wired. And God has great things to say about how relationships work—and don't work. By putting biblical truths into practical, hands-on skills, teenagers will learn what it means to live as the body of Christ. Through intentional friend making, they'll experience God's love and friendship with them.

- **Friendship First makes only one assumption—that we can't make any assumptions!** That may sound goofy, but we do know that many people—even Christians—don't know the basics of the Christian faith! So we've boiled down friendship (with others and Jesus) to practical, simple concepts. In doing so, we found that some of the simplest messages are the most profound. Simple doesn't mean simplistic.

SIMPLE ≠ SIMPLISTIC

We didn't assume that people know basic relational skills either. So we started with step-by-step ways to learn how to be a friend.

- **We believe less is more.** Friendship takes time. It's more like cooking with a Crock-Pot than a microwave. Thirteen weeks may seem like a long time to devote to this series, but it's really only the beginning. Building trusting friendships with others—and God—is a lifelong process, not an instant one. Let relationships marinate.

"There is so much more I want to tell you, but you can't bear it now."—Jesus
(John 16:12)

- **We believe in "giving" relationships.** While researching for this project, we were amazed at the lack of practical friendship resources. What surprised us even more were the books about relationship building that focused on what you will "get" out of a relationship, not what you can give—books written to hone your skills so you can persuade people to think, say, and do what you want them to, and books about how to *get* the sale, *get* more dates, or *get* invited to more parties. Selfish motives.

   Friendship First immerses everyone in a God-focused perspective on friendship. It's about the joy in being the giver in a friendship—not the getter. And guess what! In the giving, you get great benefits, too.

- *Teenagers aren't objects or projects.* They're real people. Even in the church, we can be guilty of viewing others not as real people, but as notches in our Bible belt or "projects" to fix. No one likes to be seen as someone's project to be "fixed." It is only God's Spirit of love that truly brings life change—and that happens as people see, hear, touch, and feel authentic faith lived through other people. This series allows real teenagers to relate with real teenagers and uncover the joys of friendship with others and Jesus.

Do Friendship First Get-Togethers Again and Again

Once they know how fun, easy, and meaningful the Get-Togethers are, teenagers will want to form new groups and experience Friendship First with other friends in fresh ways. Our hope is that your teenagers will form spinoff groups with other friends and lead these groups themselves! Remind teenagers to invite all their friends to Get-Togethers, and encourage them to also be thinking of new circles of friends to try Friendship First with.

■ The Friendship First Recipe for Success

Think of Friendship First as a treasured family recipe. Each activity is there for a reason. And because of the people, Friendship First is distinct and fresh every time you follow "the recipe," so you can experience the get-togethers again and again. Since every small group is unique, you'll be amazed again and again at fresh discoveries. Guaranteed!

Our Prayer For You

As you embark on this life-changing adventure of friendships, we offer a prayer in Ephesians (from *The Message* by Eugene H. Peterson).

"I couldn't stop thanking God for you—every time I prayed, I'd think of you and give thanks. But I do more than thank. I ask—ask the God of our Master, Jesus Christ, the God of glory—to make you intelligent and discerning in knowing him personally, your eyes focused and clear, so that you can see exactly what it is he is calling you to do, grasp the immensity of this glorious way of life he has for Christians, oh, the utter extravagance of his work in us who trust him…

"…At the center of all this, Christ rules the church. The church, you see, is not peripheral to the world; the world is peripheral to the church. The church is Christ's body, in which he speaks and acts, by which he fills everything with his presence."

May God richly bless your efforts!

Friends in Christ,

Thom Schultz

Joani Schultz

Thom and Joani Schultz

GET-TOGETHER 1

Make friendship with Jesus and others a priority.

LUKE 10:38-42

Deadlines. Family. Laundry. Yardwork.

The to-do list of life seems unending. With so many competing priorities, it's no wonder people can often relate to the words from a favorite hymn—"weak and heavy laden, cumbered with a load of care"! As we frantically go from one chore to another, knocking them off our to-do lists, our relationships with Jesus and others suffer, and we find ourselves harried, worried, and often depressed.

Surely that's not what Jesus intends for us. Our Best Friend wants us to have joyful, abundant lives! And when we make friendship with him our number-one priority, that's exactly what we'll experience. In this Get-Together, you'll learn how to make friendships with God and others a priority.

Get-Together at a Glance

	WHAT PEOPLE WILL DO	MINUTES	SUPPLIES
CAFÉ TIME	Eat a snack or meal that connects with today's point. OPTIONS *(Choose One)*: ☐ *Quick and Easy:* Trail Mix ☐ *Easy Plus:* Ice-Cream-Sundae Bar ☐ *High Impact:* Salad Bar	10 to 15 30 60	See pp. 167-168 for details
EXPERIENCING FRIENDSHIP	*Two-Minute Mingle* Mingle and tell each other stories about friends they've had.	10 to 12	• *Friendship First* CD • CD player
	Two Approaches to Friendship Listen to the story of Mary and Martha on the CD, and discuss their different approaches to developing friendships.	10 to 12	• *Friendship First* CD • CD player
	Priority 1: Friendship Receive their Friendship First books, talk about making friendship Get-Togethers a priority, and discuss ways to make their friendships with God and others a priority in their daily lives.	10 to 12	• *Friendship First* books (one for each person) • pens • 168-inch length of string • 1 sticky note (1½ inches wide) • newsprint or white board • marker
PRAYER	Hear an affirming prayer for each member of the group.	5 to 10	
DAILY CHALLENGE	Choose a Daily Challenge.	up to 5	• *Friendship First* books • 7-inch piece of string for each person

Café Time

What friendship doesn't include eating together? Food is a very important part of the Friendship First experience. As we eat together, we grow closer together—we relax, we smile, we share. It's the perfect beginning to each friendship Get-Together. Remember that during these Get-Togethers, your focus is on people. Take the time to enjoy the fellowship of the table together.

We've provided three delicious options for each week's Get-Together. Choose the one that best fits your time, your setting, and your budget. See pages 167-168 for details on today's menu options.

PURPOSE

Each ingredient of today's food options offers something unique to the taste. In the same way, each person brings something unique to the Friendship First group of friends.

☐ **QUICK AND EASY**
Trail Mix

or

☐ **EASY PLUS**
Ice-Cream-Sundae Bar

or

☐ **HIGH IMPACT**
Salad Bar

Music IDEAS

Set a great atmosphere by playing background music that matches the mood of this Get-Together! Here are some genre suggestions:
- light jazz
- acoustic folk music
- light classical
- upbeat pop

You can also play the Friendship First theme song, "Here for You" (track 11 on the *Friendship First* CD).

HERE'S WHAT TO DO

- Make sure that each person feels welcome and at home at today's Get-Together. You may personally welcome each person, or if you'll be busy getting the last-minute details organized, find a warm, friendly person to be the greeter.

- Provide name tags for everyone.

- As each new person arrives, introduce him or her to those who are already there.

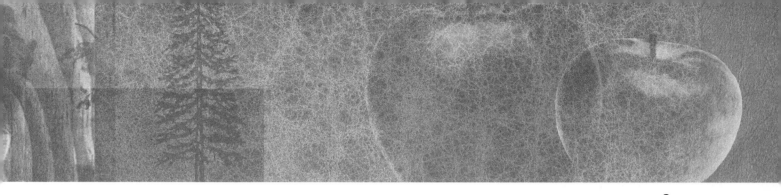

- If you're using the **Quick and Easy** or **Easy Plus** option, invite people to get a snack before they sit down in their groups of six. If you're using the High Impact option, wait to serve the food until everyone's seated.

- Enjoy getting to know all of the participants while you're waiting for everyone to arrive. Then formally welcome everyone to the first Friendship First Get-Together.

- Join together for a prayer to bless the food and your time together.

- Invite everyone to go through the buffet line and prepare a salad.

- While everyone's eating, allow for small talk and casual chatting.

- After a few minutes of discussion,

SAY **Welcome to our first Get-Together. I'm so glad that you've all come to Friendship First. We'll be meeting once a week for the next 12 weeks to talk about deepening our relationships. We'll do a lot of fun things to become good friends. But we have a higher purpose too—everything that we do together will help us explore the idea that the process of becoming friends with one another is very similar to the process of becoming friends with God. Keep that idea tucked in the back of your mind as we talk and enjoy one another's company.**

- Break the ice by playing this name game: Have each person say his or her first name and tell a true story that goes along with the name. For example, perhaps Carol was a Christmas baby and was named for Christmas carols, or perhaps Tom's real name is Eugene, but he chooses to go by Tom because it was his favorite uncle's name. Go ahead and tell your name "story."

SAY **That was fun! Sharing stories is a great way to get to know others. Eating is a great thing to do together with new friends too. Each week the food that we eat will tie in to the topic we're discussing.**

Between Friends

Remember, friend-making is a priority at these Get-Togethers! Don't fall into the "Martha" trap of forgetting people's needs.

INSIDE SCOOP At our field test, we invited the person whose first name started closest to the letter A to go first when we played the name game. As it turned out, that person was the most shy, introverted one of the group and was uncomfortable going first. We suggest, instead, that you ask for volunteers to go first with this game, and then encourage everyone else to jump in with their own story once they feel comfortable sharing.

GET-TOGETHER

1

*Make friendship
with Jesus and others
a priority.*

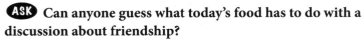

ASK Can anyone guess what today's food has to do with a discussion about friendship?

SAY Those are all great ideas! It took lots of different ingredients to make these great meals (or snacks). If you think about it, our group here today is kind of like a multi-ingredient meal (or snack). We all offer something unique to this mix of friends.

• Have people form pairs.

• Have one person in each pair take one minute to discover as much as he or she can about the other person and be prepared to introduce the partner to the rest of the group.

• After a minute, have the other person in each pair take a minute to discover as much as possible about the partner.

• Have people take turns introducing their new friends to the rest of the group.

EXPERIENCING Friendship

Two-Minute Mingle

1

In this activity, the participants will enjoy sharing stories about their friends and getting to know the other participants better. It will also help people learn how to mingle in a fun, non-threatening environment.

HERE'S WHAT TO DO

- You'll need an open space for "mingling." You may need to move tables and chairs to create an environment for lots of interaction.

- Cue the *Friendship First* CD to the "Two-Minute Mingle Music," track 1.

- Have everyone gather in the open space for this fun, two-minute mingling game. Have each person stand next to a new friend.

  SAY **First, say hello to your new friend, and tell your friend how glad you are that he or she is here.** (Pause.)

- Start the music, and have the person in each pair who's wearing the most blue tell his or her partner a story about a childhood friend.

- After one minute, call out, "Switch!" Have the other person tell about a childhood friend.

- After one minute, flash the lights. Have everyone mingle and find a new friend.

- When everyone's paired up again, give pairs a new topic to discuss:
  Tell a story about a friend from junior high or high school.

- After one minute, call out, "Switch!"

- After another minute, switch the lights off and on so everyone knows it's time to find another new partner.

- Give the new topic:
  Tell a story about a best friend you have now.

Getting to know one another during the two-minute mingle.

INSIDE SCOOP At our field test, some people had a little trouble finding new partners during this activity—they wanted to chat with the same person rather than talk to someone new. But this game is designed to help people become comfortable making conversation with new friends. Watch the group and be ready to guide people to new partners.

- After one minute, call out, "Switch!"
- When the music comes to an end, have everyone find a chair and form a tight, knee-to-knee circle.
- Discuss this question:

ASK **What did you discover during our mingling activity?**

SAY **Think about the stories you told about your friends, as well as what you've just experienced in getting to know some new friends.**

- Discuss these questions:

ASK **What draws us to be friends with others?**

How are the things that draw us to our friends like the same things that draw us to explore a relationship with God? Explain.

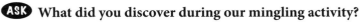

Two Approaches to Friendship

In this activity, people will explore the story of Mary and Martha and make discoveries about how to make friendships with others and God a priority.

HERE'S WHAT TO DO

SAY **Let's listen to a story that illustrates friendship. The story is about two women who are entertaining a friend who happens to be a very important and influential person.**

- Play "Mary and Martha Drama," track 2 on the *Friendship First* CD.

- Discuss these questions:

ASK **What were you thinking and feeling as you heard this story?**

As you think about each of these three friends, what do you think their words and actions say about their relationships with each other?

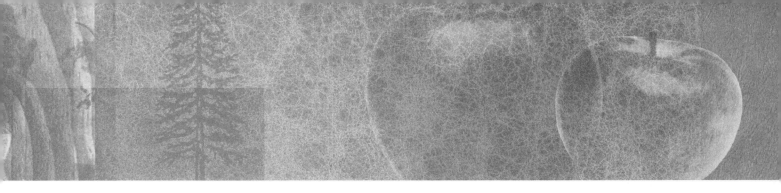

SAY This story is true—it's recorded in the Bible and is about a time Jesus visited two sisters, Mary and Martha, in their home.

- Read aloud the biblical account in Luke 10:38-42.

- Discuss these questions:

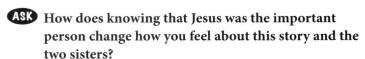

ASK How does knowing that Jesus was the important person change how you feel about this story and the two sisters?

What message do you believe Jesus is giving when he says that "There is only one thing worth being concerned about"?

Priority 1: Friendship

This activity will help people explore the priority of friendship.

HERE'S WHAT TO DO

- Give each person a *Friendship First* book, and tell people to bring the books with them each week.

SAY During our time together, this book will guide us along our journey as we discover that making friends with God is a lot like making friends with people.

- Have everyone turn to page 11 and write a "to-do" list for the week on that page.

SAY Take a look at your to-do list and all of the things that you'll spend time on this week. Now, imagine yourself years from now—just before your natural death.

Think to yourself about which of the entries on your list you'll be glad you did. Which stand out as proud markers of your life? Which won't matter? (Pause for a moment of reflection.)

Participants discover the priority they give to relationships with God and others.

- Show the group the 168-inch piece of string or rope that you prepared before the Get-Together. Have two people in the group hold the ends of the string so that it's pulled taut.

  SAY **This length of string represents one week's worth of time. There are 168 hours in a week, and each inch represents an hour in your week.** Wrap a sticky note around the string. **This sticky note is about 1½ inches wide. It represents the time we've committed to each week for 13 weeks to deepen our friendship with one another and God.**

- Have everyone stand up and spread out along the length of string. Ask people to estimate how much time they actually spend developing relationships with others. Have people simply pinch a length of the string between their fingers to show their best guesses.

- Have participants talk with the people standing on both sides of them about why they spend that much or that little time developing their relationships. Also have them talk about the quality versus quantity issue in regard to the time they spend developing relationships.

- Discuss this question:

  ASK **What do you think the goal of friendship is? How do we reach that goal?**

  SAY **Now, think about growing a friendship with God. If becoming friends with God is similar to becoming friends with people, think about how much time you think it would take on a weekly basis to become good friends with God. Pinch a length of string to show how much time you think it'd take. Then talk to the people on both sides of you about what you think about this idea that making friends with God is similar to making friends with people.**

- Invite everyone to take a seat again. Put away the string. Invite volunteers to share their insights with the rest of the group.

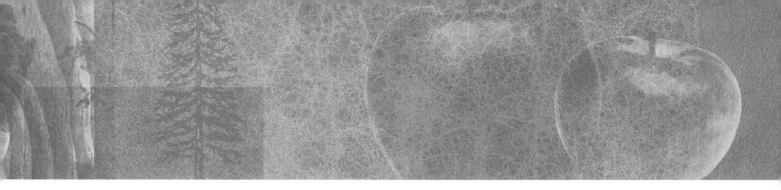

SAY These Get-Togethers will help us practice making friendships a priority. Let's talk about how we'll do that. Look at the list on this page. Let's take turns reading those items aloud.
Pause to read aloud.

ASK These are pretty good ground rules for our Get-Togethers. Is there anything else we should add to this core list?

- Take no more than three minutes to write everyone's ideas on a sheet of newsprint or on a white board. Here are some possible additional ground rules to discuss.

- Attendance—Everyone agrees to make the Get-Togethers a priority. If there's an emergency, let someone know you can't make it.

- Confidentiality—What is said within the group stays within the group. The group should be a safe place to share.

- Openness—Everyone tries to not be judgmental, even if he or she strongly disagrees. Instead, people will learn how to discuss and grow from disagreements.

- Participation—Everyone participates. Shy people can make an effort to be involved. Talkers can make an effort to be better listeners.

SAY It's important for us to remember to be considerate of one another. We're in this together! It matters how we treat one another. It also matters that we spend time together.

It'll be tough for us to become friends with each other if we only meet or talk once a week. Let's have an autograph party. Everyone autograph everyone else's book with phone number, e-mail, and street address so we can connect other times during the week.

- Have everyone first write his or her own name in the space provided and then rotate books from person to person.

We talk.
We help each other.
We laugh.
We do stuff together.
We invest time with each other.
We're open.
We accept each other, warts and all.
We have fun together.
We build each other up.
We listen.
We trust each other.
We sympathize with each other.
We give and take advice.
We keep each other accountable.
We forgive.
We keep confidences.
We respect each other.
We commit to each other.

Sharing phone numbers and e-mail addresses helps everyone become friends outside the Get-Together.

Prayer

Take the opportunity to affirm others by praying aloud for each member of the group. This is a great way to model praying aloud for those who may be uncomfortable doing it themselves.

HERE'S WHAT TO DO

• Have everyone in the group stand and hold hands for this open-eye prayer.

PRAY Move around the circle, and pray aloud for each person. For example you might pray, "Lord, thank you for our time together getting to know Merrie. Thank you for her sweet spirit. God, please bless her as she seeks to deepen her relationships with others and with you."

Prayer brings participants closer together.

Daily Challenge™

The Daily Challenge will give people an opportunity to practice what they explored during the week's Get-Together.

HERE'S WHAT TO DO

- Have everyone turn to page 127 in the *Friendship First* book. Have a volunteer read the "Make Friendship a Priority" Daily Challenges aloud.

- Have everyone choose one of the challenges to do in the coming week and mark it in the book. Ask people to take turns around the room telling which challenge they plan to do.

- Tell everyone to be ready to report how the Daily Challenge went next time they meet.

- Give each person a seven-inch piece of string as a reminder of the challenge to make friendships a priority each day of the week. The piece of string can be used as a bookmark in the book.

- Encourage everyone to read Chapter 1 of the *Friendship First* book during the week.

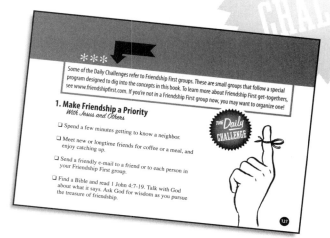

GET-TOGETHER
2

Go beyond first impressions with Jesus and others.

JOHN 15:15

First impressions, whether positive or negative, are very powerful. Negative impressions may lead to misconceptions that prevent good friendships from developing. In this Get-Together, participants will focus on putting aside misconceptions of others and Jesus. They will also discover how to grow a vital, intimate friendship by being genuinely interested and truly themselves—100 percent authentic!

Get-Together at a Glance

	WHAT PEOPLE WILL DO	MINUTES	SUPPLIES
 **CAFÉ TIME**	Eat a snack or meal that connects with today's point. OPTIONS *(Choose One):* ☐ *Quick and Easy:* Cornflakes Surprise ☐ *Easy Plus:* Gelatin Drinks ☐ *High Impact:* Meatloaf Cake	 10 to 15 30 60	See pp. 169-170 for details
 **EXPERIENCING FRIENDSHIP**	***Digging In*** Use *Friendship First* books to role-play scenarios in pairs, and discuss how intentionally friendly and open conversation leads to authentic friendship.	10 to 12	• *Friendship First* books (1 per person) • pens or pencils
	Hello, This Is Me Explore what they offer and want in friendships.	10 to 12	• *Friendship First* books • pens or pencils
	Friends of God Discover ways to put aside misconceptions of God and build intimate friendship with Jesus.	10 to 12	• Bibles • *Friendship First* books • pens or pencils
 **PRAYER**	Use an object in a prayer, and reflect on a song that expresses a desire to grow closer to God.	5 to 10	• CD player • *Friendship First* CD
 **DAILY CHALLENGE**	Talk about the Daily Challenges they'll carry out during the week.	up to 5	• *Friendship First* books

*W*hat friendship doesn't
include eating together?
*Food is a very important part of
the Friendship First experience. As
we eat together, we grow closer
together—we relax, we smile,
we share. It's the perfect beginning
to each friendship Get-Together.
Remember that during these
Get-Togethers, your focus is on
people. Take the time to enjoy the
fellowship of the table together.*

*We've provided three delicious
options for each week's Get-
Together. Choose the one that
best fits your time, your setting,
and your budget. See pages
169-170 for details on today's
menu options.*

Music IDEAS

Set a great atmosphere by playing
background music that matches the
mood of this Get-Together! Here are
some genre suggestions:
  • light pop
  • rap
  • Latin
  • jazz
You can also play the Friendship First
theme song, "Here for You" (track 11
on the *Friendship First* CD).

Café Time

PURPOSE
*Food that looks like one thing but is actually something else
will lead into discussion of first impressions.*

☐ *QUICK AND EASY*
Cornflakes Surprise

or

☐ *EASY PLUS*
Gelatin Drinks

or

☐ *HIGH IMPACT*
Meatloaf Cake

HERE'S WHAT TO DO

• Make sure that each person feels welcome and at home at today's
Get-Together. You may personally welcome each person, or if
you'll be busy getting the last-minute details organized, find a
warm, friendly person to be the greeter.

• If you're using the **Quick and Easy** or **Easy Plus** option, invite
people to get a snack before they sit down in their groups of six.

• If you're using the **High Impact** option, wait until
everyone's arrived.

• Join together for a prayer to bless the food and your time together.

• Have everyone fill a plate, sit down, and begin eating.

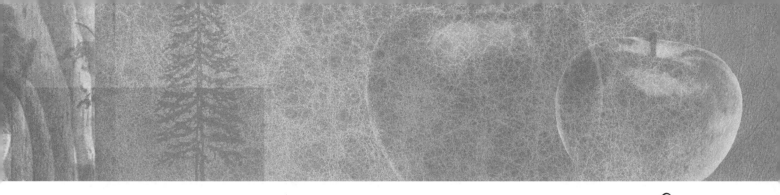

- While everyone's eating, allow for small talk and casual chatting.

- At some point in the conversation, discuss Chapter 1 in the *Friendship First* book. Ask people what struck them most about what they read.

- After a few minutes of discussion (or when there's a natural break in the conversation), discuss the significance of the food.

ASK **What could the food we're eating today symbolize about friendship? Let's think of as many possibilities as we can.**

SAY **Thanks for all your ideas! As you can see, the food we're enjoying looks like one thing but is actually something totally different. Our meal today offers us some surprises once we dig into it. Today we're going to talk about first impressions. We're going to explore what it means to build friendships that go beyond first impressions, and we'll discuss how misconceptions often prevent us from really getting to know people and God.**

First let's check in on the Daily Challenges. How did you follow through with your Daily Challenge commitment, and what happened as a result?

- Thank everyone for sharing a Daily Challenge story.

SAY **As I mentioned earlier, today we're discussing first impressions and the ways we're often surprised by people when we get to know them.**

- Discuss these questions:

ASK **When have you been surprised by someone once you "dug into" a friendship?**

Why has it been a challenge or struggle to go beyond your first impression of someone?

Between Friends

This discussion will work equally well for the Gelatin Drinks and Meatloaf Cake, since they must be actually touched (so they fit the questions about "digging in"). The surprise in the Cornflakes Surprise comes when people pour colored milk out of the cartons. If you choose this food option, you may want to adjust the discussion to touch more on visual surprise. For instance, when have they felt a jolt of surprise when beginning a friendship?

Also, if you choose the Gelatin Drinks option, wait until everyone has discovered that the gelatin is not, in fact, liquid. (They may discover this by stirring with the straw or moving the glass, for example). Then get out the actual beverages, cups, and spoons.

**EXPERIENCING
Friendship**

Between Friends

If anyone has already completed any of these activities from the *Friendship First* book, they'll still find value in thinking further, writing more, or adding to what they did earlier. Encourage everyone to participate, whether people are completely new to these book experiences or not.

INSIDE SCOOP

In our experience, teenagers were much more comfortable doing the "Digging In" activity in pairs rather than in the small groups. We're often much more comfortable discussing and trying things with one other person than with a larger number.

Also, have pairs act out the Hal Hopper exercise together because, even if they understood the meaning as they read the book, true significance emerges best in hands-on experience. Reading about something and actually experiencing it are two different things—and it's during the experience that life-changing discovery takes place.

Digging In

In this activity, people will practice conversational skills and discover how to develop more authentic friendships.

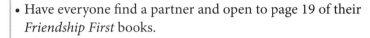

HERE'S WHAT TO DO

- Have everyone find a partner and open to page 19 of their *Friendship First* books.

- Ask pairs to read together the "Good First Impressions" section (emphasize that they should not yet continue on to the next section, "Be You.")

- Have pairs discuss these questions:

   ASK **What points about good first impressions do you agree or disagree with? Why?**

  How might intentionally making a good first impression prevent some of the struggles we mentioned earlier?

- Now have pairs read together the "Small Talk" section beginning on page 21 of the *Friendship First* book. Afterward, help pairs debrief with an activity that will combine the two chapter sections in a practical and creative way.

  SAY **With your partner, you'll practice an encounter that follows the Hal Hopper exercise step by step *and* includes the friendly signals. You'll be able to see for yourselves how both might help build a friendship.**

- Give people directions for the Hal Hopper exercise:

  Each partner should choose one of the four friendly signals—smile, look approachable; look people in the eye; shake hands—and focus on doing it in the "first impression" scenario. (This signal can be something they already do when meeting someone, or it can be something they've just now discovered and want to begin concentrating on.)

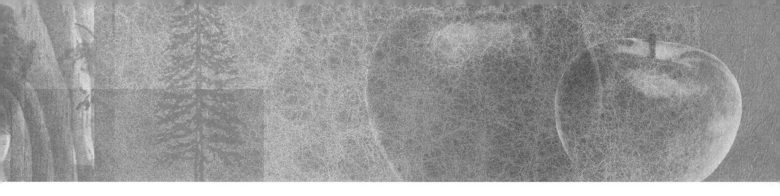

- Partners should then take turns going through the Hal Hopper steps.

- Have partners go through the Hal Hopper steps focusing on one of the signals.

FOR DEEPER IMPACT

Add a twist to this activity by having pairs first go through the Hal Hopper steps with a deliberate misuse of the friendly signals. These should be ridiculous and funny, not personally offensive. For instance, someone might bestow on his or her partner overly exaggerated and phony laughter, while someone else might show an over-the-top lack of interest (staring at the ceiling and muttering "Mmm…," answering a cell phone during the conversation, or spontaneously breaking into song). You could also suggest mimicking other things people have done to them that really communicated disinterest. Encourage pairs to have some fun with this but to also consider how what they're doing connects with their real-life experiences. Afterward, you'll have a great opportunity to discuss how frustrating it is when people treat you with disrespect or aren't genuine.

- Call time after two or three minutes.

- Discuss these questions:

 ASK **What did you discover during this experience? Explain.**

How is this like or unlike getting acquainted with Jesus?

- Have each person go to the cornflakes-box activity on page 21 of the *Friendship First* book.

- Participants should design a cover for the cornflakes box as if they were "advertising" themselves. Encourage them to include what first impressions or conceptions people might have about them. The first impressions can be positive or negative, accurate or inaccurate.

 INSIDE SCOOP When we did this activity, pairs wouldn't stop talking! People who didn't know each other before the activity went beyond the conversation steps, and people who already knew each other connected in new ways. This exercise proves the power of basic and simple experiences!

 INSIDE SCOOP The question that connects getting acquainted with Jesus to getting acquainted with others may seem like a stretch—but it's not! Someone in our group mentioned that although we may not think we need to be "introduced" to God in the same way (name, where do you live, and so on), it's very important that we learn and understand the many different names of Jesus, the things Jesus cares about, and so on.

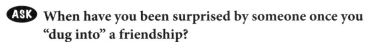

- Afterward, have people form pairs and discuss:

ASK **When have you been surprised by someone once you "dug into" a friendship?**

Why has it been a challenge or struggle to go beyond your first impression of someone?

SAY **Let's go even deeper now by taking a look at some of our own personal hopes, fears, and longings about friendship.**

Hello, This Is Me

This activity will help people think more deeply about who they really are and what God thinks of them.

HERE'S WHAT TO DO

Between Friends

If you chose the first food option for today's Get-Together, keep the box of cornflakes nearby. Display the box while pairs design their personal cereal-box labels. Even if you chose another food option, you can still bring in and display a cornflakes box. A visual example will provide inspiration and jump-start ideas.

- Direct people to find a space away from others where they can spend time in individual reflection.

- Have everyone return to the cornflakes-box activity on page 21 of the *Friendship First* book.

- This time, they should fill in an ingredients label for the side of the cornflakes box. They should write the "inside ingredients" that make up the real person.

- Encourage people to be transparent during this experience and use it as a "self-disclosure" regarding what they offer in friendship. (Also, remind people to allow what they think and write to flow out of the activities and discussions you've had today.)

- After a couple minutes, have people form pairs to discuss the label activity.

- Ask the following questions, pausing between questions so people can answer with their partners.

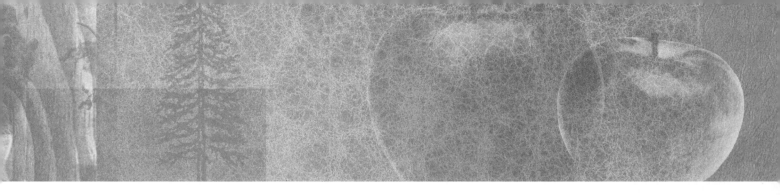

 ASK What do the things you wrote say about the real you?

How do you think Jesus might fill in your ingredients label?

3 Friends of God

This activity will encourage everyone to put aside misconceptions about Jesus and grow closer to him.

HERE'S WHAT TO DO

- Have a volunteer read John 15:15 aloud.

- Discuss these questions:

  ASK What emotions or thoughts does this verse stir in you? Explain.

  What does it mean to you that God wants to call you friend and not slave?

- Ask everyone to turn to page 28 in the *Friendship First* book and fill in the empty cloud with first impressions or misconceptions they may have of God. Play the *Friendship First* song "Here for You" (track 11) on the *Friendship First* CD.

  SAY Now, based on what you've discovered today through our experiences and this Scripture verse, go back and cross out the words that no longer accurately describe your view of God.

- Discuss these questions:

  ASK In what ways will you put aside these crossed-out misconceptions and get to know Jesus as your most intimate friend?

  How would a growing friendship with Jesus affect your other relationships?

GET-TOGETHER 2

Go beyond first impressions with Jesus and others.

Between Friends

Participants will take these objects home, so encourage them to choose items from their own possessions or from common group supplies (such as pens, paper, or tape). You might also bring in additional objects for people to choose from—such as candles, small rocks, or sunglasses.

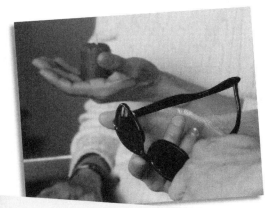

Participants pray about building intimacy with Jesus in specific ways.

Prayer

This prayer activity will help people surrender their first impressions and see themselves and others through God's eyes.

HERE'S WHAT TO DO

SAY Now let's spend a few moments praying—surrendering some things to God and asking for help. To make our prayers and commitments more tangible, I'd like everyone to quickly find one object that represents something that's preventing you from pursuing an intimate friendship with a person or Jesus. You can find an object either in the room or in your pockets, bag, wallet, or purse. For instance, you might choose a dollar bill to symbolize a misconception that God is an impersonal friend who cares only about performance and success. Or you might choose a schedule or calendar to represent your commitment to find the time and opportunity to genuinely get acquainted with others and with God.

As you pray silently, hold your object as a way of confessing your struggles or presenting your desire to build an intimate friendship with Jesus—which will overflow into friendships with others. Once you've expressed this to God, set down the object as a way of committing your struggle or desire to his care—and thank him that you can rely on him to be your best friend!

- Give people just a few moments to find an object.

- Play "I Surrender to You" by Jeremy Camp, track 3 on the *Friendship First* CD, and have people reflect on the words and message of the song as they pray.

- Once everyone has finished praying silently, close with a prayer.

PRAY God, thank you for making each of us unique and valuable. Help us put aside misconceptions of others and build intimate, lasting friendships. Show us also how to get rid of any first impressions of Jesus that are preventing us from experiencing the best of all friendships, and help us get to know who Jesus really is. Amen.

Daily Challenge™

The Daily Challenge will give people an opportunity to practice what they explored during the week's Get-Together.

HERE'S WHAT TO DO

- Have everyone go to page 128 of the *Friendship First* book. Have a volunteer read the "Go Beyond First Impressions" Daily Challenges aloud.

- Have everyone choose one of the challenges to do in the coming week and mark it in the *Friendship First* book. Ask people to take turns around the room telling which challenge they plan to do.

- Tell everyone to be ready to report how the Daily Challenge went next time the group meets.

- Encourage everyone to continue reading Chapter 2 of the *Friendship First* book throughout the week.

- Have people take home their prayer objects to remind them of their commitments to put aside first impressions and to genuinely get acquainted with others and with Jesus. Everyone should use this object as a tangible reminder to follow through on the Daily Challenge.

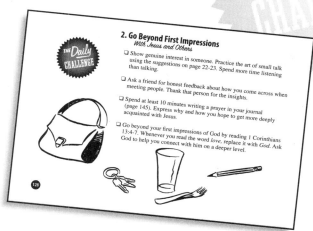

GET-TOGETHER

3

Experience love with Jesus and others.

1 JOHN 4:7-8

Isn't love what all of us want more than anything else? To know that we're loved even though we're not always very lovable. That's what our Best Friend gives to us.

Jesus loves us all day, every day. His love shows itself in the beautiful world he gave us to live in. He loves us by providing for our needs, by healing our hurts, by planning good things for our lives, by offering us eternal friendship. Amazing, wonderful love—that's what he gives!

And, in turn, we respond by loving him and by showing his love to others! It's a pretty fantastic plan!

Get-Together at a Glance

	WHAT PEOPLE WILL DO	MINUTES	SUPPLIES
CAFÉ TIME	Eat a snack or meal that connects with today's point. OPTIONS *(Choose One)*: ☐ *Quick and Easy:* Heart-Shaped Cookies ☐ *Easy Plus:* Heart-Shaped Muffins ☐ *High Impact:* Heart-Shaped Pizza	10 to 15 30 60	See pp. 171-172 for details
EXPERIENCING FRIENDSHIP	*Random Story* Watch a DVD segment to see how God showed love to one family.	5 to 10	• *Friendship First* DVD • TV and DVD player
	Our Stories Share how God has shown his love with them.	30 to 40	• *Friendship First* books (1 per person) • watch or clock
	A Time and Place Meditate on God's love.	5 to 10	• *Friendship First* CD • CD player • *Friendship First* books • pens
PRAYER	Acknowledge God's love for them in prayer.	5 to 10	
DAILY CHALLENGE	Talk about the Daily Challenges they'll carry out during the week.	up to 5	• *Friendship First* books • small paper heart for each person

Café Time

What friendship doesn't include eating together? Food is a very important part of the Friendship First experience. As we eat together, we grow closer together—we relax, we smile, we share. It's the perfect beginning to each friendship Get-Together. Remember that during these Get-Togethers, your focus is on people. Take the time to enjoy the fellowship of the table together.

We've provided three delicious options for each week's Get-Together. Choose the one that best fits your time, your setting, and your budget. See pages 171-172 for details on today's menu options.

Music IDEAS

Set a great atmosphere by playing background music that matches the mood of this Get-Together! Here are some genre suggestions:

- oldies
- light classical
- romantic
- instrumental music

You can also play the Friendship First theme song, "Here for You" (track 11 on the *Friendship First* CD).

PURPOSE

Today's lesson is about love. All of the food has a valentine theme.

☐ *QUICK AND EASY*
Heart-Shaped Cookies

or

☐ *EASY PLUS*
Heart-Shaped Muffins

or

☐ *HIGH IMPACT*
Heart-Shaped Pizza

HERE'S WHAT TO DO

- Make sure that each person feels welcome and at home at today's Get-Together. You may personally welcome each person, or if you'll be busy getting the last-minute details organized, find a warm, friendly person to be the greeter.

- If you're using the **Quick and Easy** or **Easy Plus** option, invite people to get a snack before they sit down in their groups of six.

- If you're using the **High Impact** option, wait until everyone's arrived.

- Join together for a prayer to bless the food and your time together.

- Have everyone fill a plate, sit down, and begin eating.

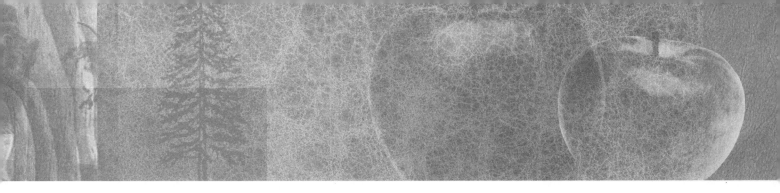

- While everyone's eating, allow for small talk and casual chatting.

- At some point in the conversation, discuss Chapter 2 in the *Friendship First* book. Ask people what struck them most in what they read.

- After a few minutes of discussion (or when there's a natural break in the conversation), discuss the significance of the food.

  ASK **What could the food we're eating today symbolize about friendship? Let's think of as many possibilities as we can.**

  SAY **Today we're talking about the love that friends have for each other, so our food is all heart-shaped for a valentine theme.**

- Discuss these questions:

  ASK **What do you remember about celebrating Valentine's Day as a child?**

- Tell us about a time in your life you felt especially well loved.

  SAY **Now let's check in on the Daily Challenges. How did you follow through with your Daily Challenge commitment, and what happened as a result?**

- Thank everyone for sharing a Daily Challenge story.

 INSIDE SCOOP Our Friendship First group included three small groups of eight meeting at the same time, so we set up the food to be served buffet style. We served the heart-shaped pizza, but when the people at the back of the food line got to the food, the pizza no longer looked like a heart. You can make sure that everyone experiences the theme of the food by decorating the table with construction paper hearts and pink or red tablecloths.

EXPERIENCING Friendship

1 Random Story

This activity will help everyone see that God does show his love to people every day.

HERE'S WHAT TO DO

- Set up the television and DVD player. Cue the DVD player to the "God's Love Revealed" segment on the *Friendship First* DVD.

SAY The Bible says, "Dear *friends*, let us continue to love one another, for love comes from God. Anyone who loves is a child of God and knows God. But anyone who does not love does not know God, for God is love" (1 John 4:7-8, emphasis added).

SAY Today we're going to have an opportunity to demonstrate love to one another, and we'll talk about how God has shown his love to us. First, let's watch a DVD clip about how God showed his love to one man.

- Show the first segment on the *Friendship First* DVD.

- After the DVD clip, discuss these questions:

ASK What did you find remarkable about this man's story?

How did God show his love in his life?

Participants watch a segment from the Friendship First DVD.

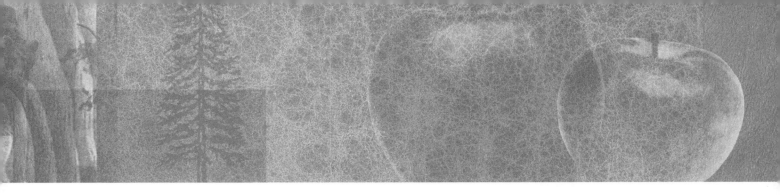

Our Stories

This activity will give all group members an opportunity to share their story and acknowledge God's loving presence in their lives. Everyone will also have a chance to hear how God has shown love to everyone else.

HERE'S WHAT TO DO

> **SAY** **Everyone has a remarkable story about how God has shown him or her love. A lot of the fun in meeting new people is discovering what is remarkable or unusual about their stories. Turn to page 24 in *Friendship First*.**

- Have someone read aloud the first paragraph under the heading "Be Interested" and the Dale Carnegie quotation next to it.

> **SAY** **Let's follow Dale Carnegie's advice as we listen to each other's stories.**

- Choose a volunteer to be the timekeeper. Make sure the volunteer has access to a clock or watch.

- Share the story of your life in three to four minutes—be sure to include how God has shown his love to you.

 INSIDE SCOOP Several people in our group were a little bit nervous about talking about themselves for four minutes. But the story shared by the discussion leader helped everyone in the group understand what kinds of things to share. The example also helped everyone see that three or four minutes isn't really that much time.

Between Friends

Provide tissues for this activity. For many, this will be a powerfully emotional time as they realize, maybe for the first time, that God has been showing love to them their entire lives.

GET-TOGETHER

3

Experience love with Jesus and others.

Between Friends

Be sure that this activity doesn't become a measure of spirituality or maturity. No one should feel that his or her experience is "less" than anyone else's. To help ensure this, choose the story you share from everyday life. In other words, this is not the time to share about how God showed his love to you by helping you bring 1,000 people to faith while preaching at a Billy Graham–type evangelistic event.

....

It's possible that some people may be truly stumped when they try to think of how God has shown love to them. Encourage these people to share how they'd like to experience God's love in the future.

- Have everyone in the group take three to four minutes to share the story of his or her life, including how God has shown his love.

- Have the timekeeper let people know when their time is almost up so they can wrap up their stories.

Note: If you have six to eight people in your group, this activity will take about 30 to 40 minutes. Don't rush through the stories, and don't leave anyone out. You'll need to keep a close eye on the time, though, so you have plenty of time for the next activity.

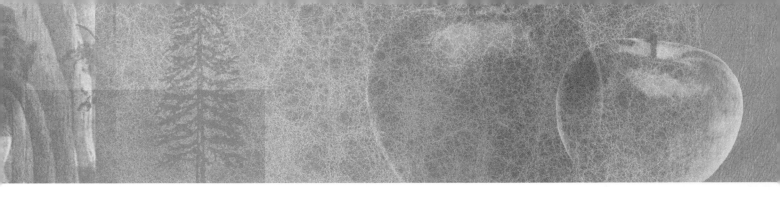

A Time and Place

3

This activity will give everyone an opportunity to meditate on God's love as expressed in Scripture.

HERE'S WHAT TO DO

SAY Get comfy and close your eyes as you listen to these words from Scripture. After the Scripture passage, there will be three minutes of quiet music. While the music plays, think about all the stories you've heard today and how each person has experienced God's love in his or her life. Think about this question: Why is God's love for us such a big deal?

• Direct group members to the valentine heart on page 30 of *Friendship First*, and invite them to write their thoughts and insights there. Provide pens.

• Play track 4 from the *Friendship First* CD. It's an interpretive reading of Romans 8:35, 37-39. Following the Scripture reading are three minutes of quiet instrumental music.

• Discuss these questions:

ASK Why do you think God's love for us is such a big deal?

What do these words from the Bible tell you about God's nature and his character?

How is experiencing love from another person like or unlike experiencing love from God?

I feel accepted when someone...

I feel unaccepted when someone...

"The Lord looks at the heart."
I Samuel 16:7

heart.

Prayer

This prayer time gives people an opportunity to show love to one another and to acknowledge God's love for them.

HERE'S WHAT TO DO

SAY **For our prayer time today, I'd like us to acknowledge that we are a circle of friends and that we're here for a specific purpose—to love each other and to see the love of God demonstrated through us to each other. Let's acknowledge that fact by standing and holding hands.** (Pause.)

Listen again to these words from Scripture:

"Dear friends, let us continue to love one another, for love comes from God. Anyone who loves is a child of God and knows God. But anyone who does not love does not know God, for God is love" (1 John 4:7-8).

SAY **Now squeeze your neighbors' hands and smile warmly at them to let them know you love them.** (Pause.)

Squeezing a friend's hand during prayer shows love and care.

• Have people think of one word that describes their feelings in response to how God has shown love to them; for example, perhaps someone feels humbled or excited.

SAY **We'll go around the circle and pray. When it's your turn, say your word aloud, then gently squeeze the hand of the person next to you so he or she knows you care and that it's his or her turn to pray. Ready? I'll go first.**

• Pray around the circle.

PRAY Then briefly close your Get-Together in prayer. Thank God for everyone in the group, and ask God to help everyone become better friends with each other and with him.

Daily Challenge™

The Daily Challenge will give people an opportunity to practice what they explored during the week's Get-Together.

HERE'S WHAT TO DO

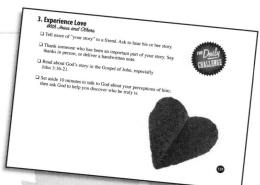

- Have everyone turn to page 129 of the *Friendship First* book. Have a volunteer read the "Experience Love" Daily Challenges aloud.

- Have everyone choose one of the challenges to do in the coming week and mark it in the book. Go around the room, and have everyone tell which challenge he or she plans to do.

- Give each person a paper heart (you can make these from pink or red construction paper) as a reminder to experience and share love in relationships.

- Tell everyone to be ready to report about the Daily Challenge next time you meet.

- Encourage everyone to read Chapter 3 of *Friendship First* during the week.

Paper hearts will remind participants to share love with others.

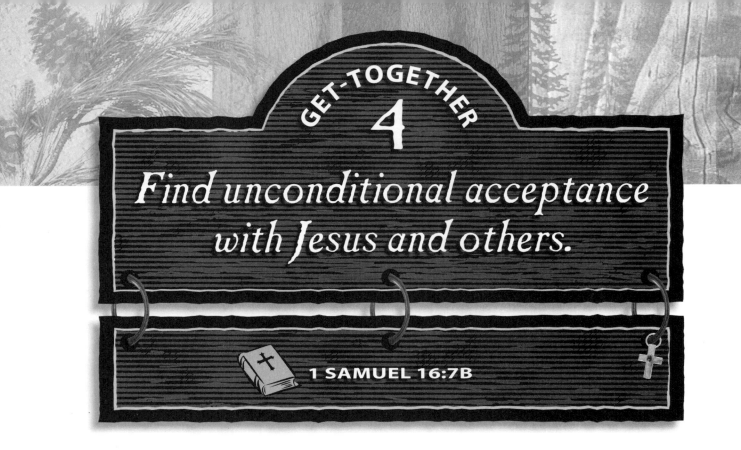

GET-TOGETHER

4

Find unconditional acceptance with Jesus and others.

1 SAMUEL 16:7B

Acceptance in friendship is a choice, and it works only when it goes both ways. In this Get-Together, participants will explore how they can both give and receive acceptance so that they may experience the greatest their friendships have to offer. In addition to seeing how others are valuable, they'll also understand their own value and respond to Jesus' amazing, unconditional acceptance.

Get-Together at a Glance

	WHAT PEOPLE WILL DO	MINUTES	SUPPLIES
 **CAFÉ TIME**	Eat a snack or meal that connects with today's point. OPTIONS *(Choose One)*: ☐ *Quick and Easy:* Bagels and Toppings ☐ *Easy Plus:* Chocolate Zucchini Cake ☐ *High Impact:* Gourmet Fast Food	 10 to 15 30 60	See pp. 173-174 for details
EXPERIENCING FRIENDSHIP	### In Common Play the "handshake" game, and talk about having things in common with others.	10 to 12	
	### The Big Picture Watch a DVD clip about rejection, and use their *Friendship First* books to explore ways they feel accepted and not accepted.	10 to 12	• *Friendship First* book for each person • *Friendship First* DVD • DVD player and TV • pens
	### For What We're Worth Explore a Scripture passage, discover God's unconditional acceptance, and affirm each other.	10 to 12	• Bibles (NLT) • Sticky notes (if possible, one pad of 1x1½-inch notes for each person) • pens
 **PRAYER**	Give over to God what's preventing them from acceptance, and respond to Jesus' offer of unconditional acceptance.	5 to 10	
 **DAILY CHALLENGE**	Talk about the Daily Challenges they'll carry out during the week.	up to 5	• *Friendship First* book for each person

GET-TOGETHER
4
Find unconditional
acceptance with
Jesus and others.

Café Time

What friendship doesn't include eating together? Food is a very important part of the Friendship First experience. As we eat together, we grow closer together—we relax, we smile, we share. It's the perfect beginning to each friendship Get-Together. Remember that during these Get-Togethers, your focus is on people. Take the time to enjoy the fellowship of the table together.

We've provided three delicious options for each week's Get-Together. Choose the one that best fits your time, your setting, and your budget. See pages 173-174 for details on today's menu options.

PURPOSE

Food with unusual ingredients or ingredients that don't seem to "belong" will lead into a discussion about acceptance.

☐ **QUICK AND EASY**
Bagels and Toppings

or

☐ **EASY PLUS**
Chocolate Zucchini Cake

or

☐ **HIGH IMPACT**
Gourmet Fast Food

HERE'S WHAT TO DO

- Make sure that each person feels welcome and at home at today's Get-Together. You may personally welcome each person, or if you'll be busy getting the last-minute details organized, find a warm, friendly person to be the greeter.

- If you're using the **Quick and Easy** or **Easy Plus** option, invite people to get a snack before they sit down in their groups of six.

- If you're using the **High Impact** option, play classical or other instrumental music to set a "sophisticated" atmosphere.

- Wait until everyone is sitting at the tables with the formal dishes and place settings, and ask the blessing.

- Serve everyone by putting fast food on the china dishes.

Music IDEAS

Set a great atmosphere by playing background music that matches the mood of this Get-Together! Here are some genre suggestions:
- romantic film
- soundtrack
- Celtic
- stirring instrumental

You can also play the *Friendship First* theme song, "Here for You" (track 11 on the *Friendship First* CD).

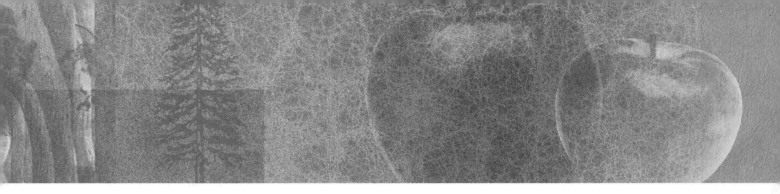

- While everyone's eating, allow for small talk and casual chatting.

- At some point in the conversation, discuss Chapter 3 in the *Friendship First* book. Ask people what struck them most in what they read.

- After a few minutes of discussion (or when there's a natural break in the conversation), discuss the significance of the food.

ASK **What could the food we're eating today symbolize about friendship? Let's think of as many possibilities as we can.**

SAY **Thanks for all your ideas! Part of what you're eating doesn't seem to quite belong. It may not be like the other parts or live up to the expectations they set. That's something many of us have felt in real life.**

Today we're going to tackle the topic of unconditional acceptance. We'll discuss what it means to be an accepting friend, and we'll explore why Jesus is the most accepting and loving friend we could have.

First let's check in on the Daily Challenges. How did you follow through with your Daily Challenge commitment, and what happened as a result?

- Thank everyone for sharing Daily Challenge stories.

SAY **Now, let's talk more about our experiences with acceptance.**

Between Friends

Tailor the discussion to your group and the food option you've chosen. For instance, all three options will lead perfectly into a conversation about feelings of belonging and not belonging, which play a role in acceptance. Discussion for the "Gourmet Fast Food" option will also touch on whether we deserve acceptance— and what it means to receive acceptance even (especially!) when we don't deserve it.

GET-TOGETHER

4

Find unconditional acceptance with Jesus and others.

EXPERIENCING
Friendship

Discovering something fun in common!

When we did this activity, the teenagers exchanged hugs instead of shaking hands. Choose a form of greeting that will work best for your group dynamics. For instance, what about high fives?

In Common

This fun, interactive game will help people experience what it's like to share (or not share!) commonalities with others.

HERE'S WHAT TO DO

SAY **We're going to play a "handshake" game. Here's how it works: I'll announce something that you might have in common with someone else in the group. You'll find a person who has that in common, and you'll shake his or her hand. OK, the first one is… find someone who's wearing the same color you're wearing!**

• Pause while people greet each other.

• Call out four or five more things people might have in common. Flash the lights in the room to get everyone's attention before calling out another commonality. Here's a list of possibilities (although you may adapt it however you'd like):

> • a birthday in the same month
>
> • a favorite television show
>
> • wearing the same kind of shoes
>
> • a sport you both play
>
> • a favorite pizza topping
>
> • a book you've just finished

• Have everyone come together to discuss these questions:

ASK **How can we relate this activity to the process of acceptance?**

SAY **Consider this statement: It's hard to completely accept people who are different from us.**

ASK **Do you agree or disagree? Why?**

When have you not been accepted because someone didn't feel like you belonged or that you deserved to belong?

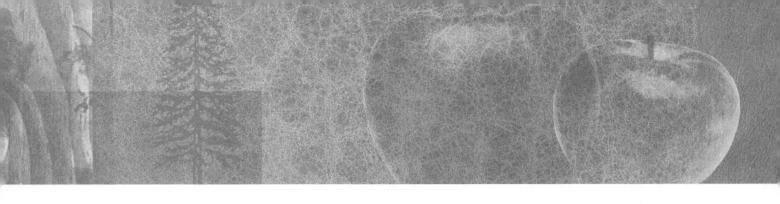

SAY For some of us, discovering "sameness" is the key to acceptance—because it's easier and more comfortable to accept people with whom we have something in common. We might feel like we deserve friends who are like us, and vice versa. For others of us, similarities don't have a huge part in how we accept people and build friendships— we have other expectations.

Friendship First™ Gathering Cards and Nature Cards are a great way to show love and concern for the people in your group. Order at www.friendshipfirst.com.

2 *The Big Picture*

This activity will help everyone understand what true acceptance is.

HERE'S WHAT TO DO

- Play "Flawed" (segment 2) on the *Friendship First* DVD.

- Have people form pairs.

- Ask these questions, pausing between each question so partners can discuss:

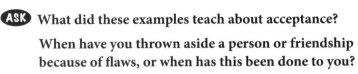

ASK **What did these examples teach about acceptance?**

When have you thrown aside a person or friendship because of flaws, or when has this been done to you?

- After people tell their stories, go to page 36 in the *Friendship First* book and read the "Signs of Acceptance" section together as a group.

- Ask everyone to complete the "I feel accepted/I feel unaccepted" activity individually.

- Have people form the same pairs to discuss these questions.

ASK **Based on your stories and answers, how would you define unconditional acceptance?**

How is unconditional acceptance like a friendship with God?

For What We're Worth

This activity will help people understand the power of God's unconditional acceptance.

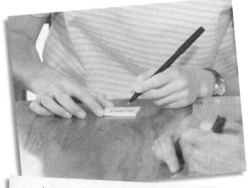

Learning about God's acceptance by writing with the "other" hand

Between Friends

When discussing unconditional acceptance, explore the difference between accepting a *person* and accepting everything that person does. Help participants understand how they can choose to accept someone because the person is valuable but not condone everything the person does. Emphasize that this is the nature of Jesus' love and acceptance for us!

HERE'S WHAT TO DO

- Gather together as a group, and have a volunteer read aloud 1 Samuel 16:7b.

- Discuss these questions:

  ASK **From this verse, what do you discover about God's acceptance for you?**

- Give a pen and a small pad of sticky notes to each person.

  SAY **Using your nondominant hand, write something good God might see when he looks at your heart. This could be a character quality, such as "compassionate" or "truthful." Or it could be something else God might value about you, such as "eager to grow" or "searching for answers."**

- Give everyone about minute to write something. Expect some chuckles.

- Discuss these questions:

  ASK **What was this experience like, and what is the end result?**

  Why is it important that the messiness and awkwardness of what you've written does not take away from its meaning?

  What might we discover about God's acceptance from this experience?

  SAY **Just as awkward writing doesn't take away from the truth and value of what we wrote, our flaws don't take away from the truth and value of who we are. God knows we're not perfect, yet he unconditionally loves and accepts each one of us.**

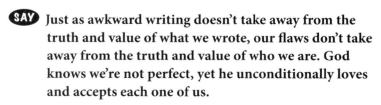

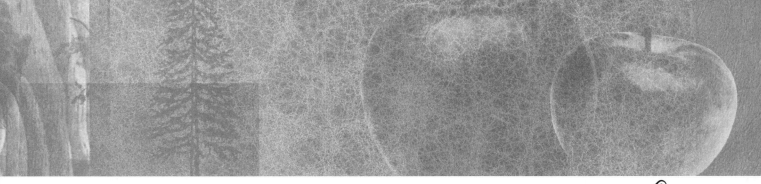

- Discuss these questions:

ASK **Why is unconditional acceptance—either giving it or receiving it—a risk?**

What effect might Jesus' unconditional acceptance have on you?

Do this activity as a way of accepting and affirming each other.

HERE'S WHAT TO DO

- Have people sit in a circle with space in the center.

SAY **Sometimes we're more aware of what's flawed about us than what's valuable about us. We need others to love and accept us for who we are. We also need others to encourage us to pursue Jesus' friendship, where we find perfect acceptance and love. So let's spend a few minutes encouraging one another. One by one, each person will get a chance to sit in the center of the circle and be "stickied." The rest of us will jot a word or phrase of encouragement for whoever is in the center—something we appreciate about that person. Then we'll stick our encouragement on him or her and say what we wrote. We'll all get an opportunity to get "stickied!"**

- Make sure everyone gets "stickied." After each person has been affirmed aloud by the others, discuss these questions:

ASK **What does this experience show about how others can help you receive Jesus' unconditional acceptance?**

How will Jesus' acceptance of you affect your friendships with others?

Between Friends

Adapt this affirmation activity to fit your group. You may want to do it in smaller groups of three or four. Or you may want the entire group to sit in a circle and have each person write only one sticky note (perhaps for the person on his or her left), which will save time and still be meaningful.

Everyone gets stickied!

 INSIDE SCOOP This was a very powerful experience in our group; teenagers were absorbed, laughing and sincerely encouraging each other. View this as a good example of how others' love and acceptance lead us to Jesus!

Prayer

In this prayer experience, people will respond to Jesus' unconditional acceptance.

HERE'S WHAT TO DO

- Have everyone point to something in the room that's about 20 feet away.

SAY Imagine that what you're pointing to is a friendship target you've been aiming at. It may be what you think you need in order to be accepted or to accept others. This is what's preventing you from unconditional acceptance.

Now, close one eye, and see how the object moves away from your finger. Open that eye, and close the other eye. Watch your target move again. Next, put your arm down, and reflect for a moment on God's love and acceptance.

We think we know the target we need to hit so that we can be fully loved and fully accepted. But Jesus is our target; Jesus never moves and offers us perfect love just as we are. Please close your eyes and pray with me.

PRAY Jesus, thank you for your unconditional acceptance and love, despite our imperfections and flaws. Please help us receive your acceptance and grow in a friendship with you. We also ask that you help us to be like you in unconditionally accepting others. Thank you. Amen.

Discovering what it's like to aim at a target that moves... unlike Jesus!

Daily Challenge™

The Daily Challenges will give people an opportunity to practice what they explored during the week's Get-Together.

HERE'S WHAT TO DO

- Have everyone go to page 130 of the *Friendship First* book. Have a volunteer read the "Find Unconditional Acceptance" Daily Challenges aloud.

- Have everyone choose one of the challenges to do in the coming week and mark it in his or her book. Ask people to take turns around the room telling which challenge they plan to do.

- Have people take home the sticky-note encouragements they received as tangible reminders to follow through on the Daily Challenge.

- Tell everyone to be ready to report how the Daily Challenge went next time the group meets.

- Encourage everyone to continue reading Chapter 3 of *Friendship First* throughout the week.

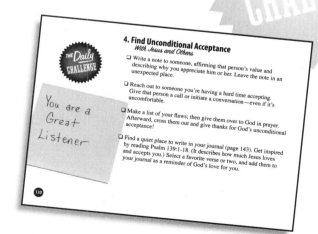

GET-TOGETHER 5

Listen to Jesus and others.

PSALM 116:1-2

Have you ever felt unheard or ignored? It's a terrible feeling that all of us have experienced. It makes us feel unvalued and unworthy. But our Best Friend is always listening to us. Jesus always has time to listen patiently and fairly to our huge problems and even our pettiest concerns. What's more, Jesus wants us to listen to him! Just as in any friendship, listening is important on both sides. Jesus' words to us are helpful, wise, and loving. Like the words of our best earthly friends, Jesus' words bring comfort. And sometimes they bring challenge because Jesus always wants the best for us. Listening to Jesus is a great habit to cultivate!

Get-Together at a Glance

CAFÉ TIME

EXPERIENCING FRIENDSHIP

PRAYER

DAILY CHALLENGE

WHAT PEOPLE WILL DO	MINUTES	SUPPLIES
Eat a snack or meal that connects with today's point. **OPTIONS** *(Choose One):*		
☐ *Quick and Easy:* Popcorn or Crunchy Granola Bars	10 to 15	See pp. 175-176 for details
☐ *Easy Plus:* Tortilla Chips and Dip	30	
☐ *High Impact:* Fritos Pie	60	
Finger-Snap Game Listen to snapping fingers to discover how hard it is to accurately listen to others.	5 to 10	
Active Listening Practice listening to each other.	5 to 10	• slips of paper and container • pen • watch or clock
Talking With Jesus Read a section in the *Friendship First* books, and discuss talking and listening to Jesus.	5 to 10	• *Friendship First* books • pens
Breathe Watch a DVD about Psalm 116:1-2 to see the connection between breathing and prayer.	5 to 10	• *Friendship First* DVD • DVD player and TV
Practice talking and listening to God as they breathe.	5 to 10	
Talk about the Daily Challenges they'll carry out during the week.	up to 5	• *Friendship First* book • sandwich bag of corn chips for each person

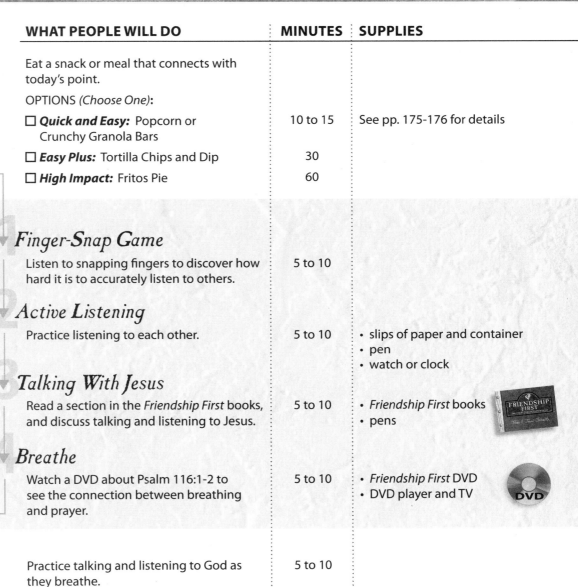

Café Time

*W*hat friendship doesn't include eating together? Food is a very important part of the Friendship First experience. As we eat together, we grow closer together—we relax, we smile, we share. It's the perfect beginning to each friendship Get-Together. Remember that during these Get-Togethers, your focus is on people. Take the time to enjoy the fellowship of the table together.

We've provided three delicious options for each week's Get-Together. Choose the one that best fits your time, your setting, and your budget. See pages 175-176 for details on today's menu options.

PURPOSE

Noisy and crunchy food will help people think about things that distract them from listening.

☐ **QUICK AND EASY**
Popcorn or Crunchy Granola Bars

or

☐ **EASY PLUS**
Tortilla Chips and Dip

or

☐ **HIGH IMPACT**
Fritos Pie

Music IDEAS

Set a great atmosphere by playing background music that matches the mood of this Get-Together! Here are some genre suggestions:

• light pop
• salsa
• Latin
• jazz

You can also play the *Friendship First* theme song, "Here for You" (track 11 on the *Friendship First* CD).

HERE'S WHAT TO DO

• Make sure that each person feels welcome and at home at today's Get-Together. You may personally welcome each person, or if you'll be busy getting the last-minute details organized, find a warm, friendly person to be the greeter.

• If you're using the **Quick and Easy** or **Easy Plus** option, invite people to get a snack before they sit down in their groups of six.

• If you're using the **High Impact** option, wait until everyone has arrived.

• Ask the blessing.

• Have everyone fill a plate, sit down, and begin eating.

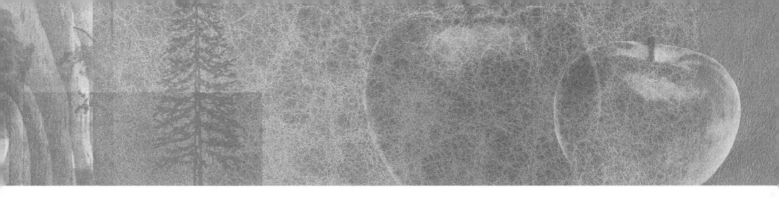

- While everyone's eating, encourage small talk and casual chatting.

- At some point in the conversation, discuss Chapter 3 in the *Friendship First* book. Ask people what struck them most from what they read.

- After a few minutes of discussion (or when there's a natural break in the conversation), discuss the significance of the food.

 ASK What could the food we're eating today symbolize about friendship? Let's think of as many ideas as possible.

SAY Today we're going to tackle the topic of listening. You may have noticed that your food was kind of crunchy and noisy to eat. We'll discuss why listening is important and how we can be good listeners. We'll also explore how to listen to God and develop a good prayer life.

 **SAY** Now let's check in on our Daily Challenges. How did you follow through with your Daily Challenge commitment? What happened as a result?

- Thank everyone for sharing a Daily Challenge story.

INSIDE SCOOP This was the week we started to notice that people knew each other well enough to share really warm and animated table conversation. People began asking about one another's personal lives and relating as friends rather than acquaintances.

EXPERIENCING Friendship

Locating the sound is more difficult than it seems!

Finger-Snap Game

In this activity, people will listen and try to pinpoint where the sound they hear is coming from. It's harder than it sounds and will help them realize that good listening requires skill.

HERE'S WHAT TO DO

- Demonstrate this activity, and explain that everyone will have a chance to try it.

- Stand behind a seated volunteer.

   SAY **I'd like you to close your eyes. All I'm going to do is snap my fingers. Please point to where the sound is coming from.**

- Imagine an arc over the volunteer's head; it's equidistant between the volunteer's ears, starting at the nose and ending at the nape of the neck. Snap your fingers several times in various places along that arc. After each snap, have the volunteer point to where the snap came from.

- Then invite the volunteer to open his or her eyes. Ask the rest of the group to give the volunteer feedback about the experiment.

   SAY **Now you'll all get a chance to try it.**

- Explain to the group how to snap in the arc that's equidistant between the ears, from the nose to the nape of the neck.

- Form pairs. Have pairs take a chair and scatter around the room.

- Ask pairs to do the activity you just demonstrated:

   One partner will sit, and the other will stand behind the chair.

   The standing partners will snap their fingers several times in places along the imaginary arc above the other partner's head.

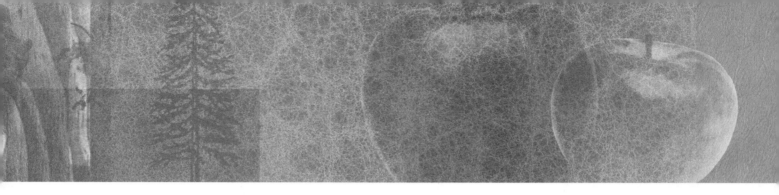

After each snap, the seated partners will point to where the sound seems to be coming from.

The standing/snapping partners will tell the seated partners how they did.

- Ask partners to switch places and play again.

- After the activity, discuss these questions:

ASK **What did you discover during this experience about the messages we send and the messages we hear?**

What insights did you gain from this experience that you can apply to listening to one another?

How can you apply these insights to listening to God?

SAY **Sometimes the message we hear is different from the message the messenger wants us to hear. Just think of all the trouble caused by people not understanding one another! Today we're going to explore the concept of listening. We'll talk about listening to each other, and we'll also talk about listening to God.**

Active Listening

This activity will help participants practice their listening skills. It'll also help them learn more about each other and deepen their friendships.

HERE'S WHAT TO DO

- Before the Get-Together, write several talk starters on slips of paper (see the list in the margin for ideas, or come up with your own). Put the slips in a container.

- Discuss this question:

ASK **What does it mean to be a good listener?**

- Form pairs, or ask people to rejoin their partners from the previous activities. Have pairs sit knee to knee.

TALK STARTERS

☐ *What always makes me laugh is...*

☐ *I'm passionate about...*

☐ *Someday I'd like to...*

☐ *A cool vacation would be to...*

☐ *My favorite thing to do with friends is...*

☐ *The best weekends always include...*

☐ *A news story that interested me recently was...*

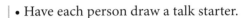

- Have each person draw a talk starter.

- Explain that one person should listen attentively while the other talks for three minutes about the subject on the talk starter.

- Call time.

- Ask partners to switch roles so that the other person listens attentively while the partner talks for three minutes.

- Call time.

- Read aloud James 1:19: **"Understand this, my dear brothers and sisters: You must all be quick to listen, slow to speak, and slow to get angry."**

- Discuss these questions:

  ASK **What was it like to be a good listener?**

  What do you appreciate about being listened to?

  What did you learn about being a good listener?

  How is listening to a friend like how God listens to us?

  SAY **Becoming close to Jesus is very much like becoming close to a friend. Listening is a big part of growing deeper friendships. We can be certain that Jesus wants to talk to us every day. Let's explore that more.**

INSIDE SCOOP We had a few very quiet people in our Friendship First group, and this was the day they really started to open up and share their thoughts and feelings with the others in the group. Could it be that being listened to helped them feel cared for and comfortable with others?

3 *Talking With Jesus*

This activity will help people think about their prayer life—the state it's in now, and how they'd like it to be.

HERE'S WHAT TO DO

- Have everyone look up page 56 in the *Friendship First* book and find the section titled "Trusting Jesus."

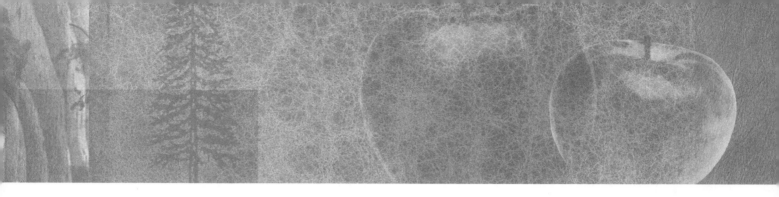

- Have someone read aloud the section that begins, "Direct communication with Jesus."

- Form pairs, and have partners discuss:

> **ASK** **What are the challenges and the rewards of talking to Jesus?**
>
> **What do you think about the idea of being silent during prayer to listen to God?**

- After a few minutes of discussion, have everyone silently fill in the spaces under "Talk With Jesus" in the book.

- Have partners discuss, in terms as general or specific as they feel comfortable with, what they'd like to say to God or have God tell them.

Breathe

This activity will help people explore Psalm 116:1-2 in a fun context. People will discover that we can be in conversation with God continually.

HERE'S WHAT TO DO

- Watch the *Friendship First* DVD segment titled "Prayer Breath."

- After the DVD segment, discuss these questions:

> **ASK** **What insights did this DVD segment give you into prayer?**
>
> **How will this DVD segment and this Get-Together change the way you pray?**

Prayer

This prayer activity will help people learn to talk and to listen while they're in conversation with God.

HERE'S WHAT TO DO

- Have everyone find a comfortable position for prayer.

  SAY **We've talked about the give-and-take of prayer today, and we've also talked about prayer in the context of breathing. So as we pray now, let's use our breath to help us learn to talk and to listen in our conversation with God.**

- Have people close their eyes, breathe out slowly, and pause for a moment when their lungs are empty. Ask them to talk silently to God as they're breathing out.

- Have people breathe in slowly and pause for a moment when their lungs are full. Ask them to listen for God during in breaths.

- Have everyone continue to breathe in this manner for three minutes—the same amount of time they spent listening to each other during the "Active Listening" activity. Tell them that you'll let them know when three minutes are up.

- After three minutes, close the Get-Together in prayer, thanking God for the privilege of talking to him any time we want to.

This practice of praying with breath builds awareness of God's voice and presence.

INSIDE SCOOP Some people in our Friendship First group found this activity deeply meaningful. Others struggled to talk and listen with each breath. Offer the option of simply sitting quietly, praying, and listening to God during these three minutes.

Daily Challenge™

The Daily Challenge will give people an opportunity to practice what they explored during the week's Get-Together.

HERE'S WHAT TO DO

- Have everyone go to page 131 of *Friendship First* book. Have a volunteer read the "Listen" Daily Challenges aloud.

- Have everyone choose one of the challenges to do in the coming week and mark it in the book. Ask people to take turns around the room telling which challenge they plan to do.

- Give everyone a small plastic bag with a few corn chips in it as a reminder to tune out the noise and listen to God and others this week.

- Tell everyone to be ready to report how the Daily Challenge went next time the group meets.

- Encourage everyone to continue reading Chapter 4 of the *Friendship First* book throughout the week.

5. Listen
to Jesus and Others

❑ Practice the listening tips on page 36. Invite a friend to share a snack, and simply listen to this friend's joys and concerns.

❑ Think of someone who needs to hear kind words from you. Ask God to give you just the right thing to say. Then let that person know how you feel.

❑ Take a walk with a friend, and bring up the idea of listening to God. Together, talk about what you think God wants you to know about your friendship with him.

❑ Turn off the TV, radio, cell phone, music—anything that makes a sound. Relax in silence and listen for God. Then slowly read Jeremiah 29:11-13. Listen for God's plan for you.

131

GET-TOGETHER

6

Find comfort in Jesus and others.

ROMANS 5:6-11

We are all broken, hurting people. Yet because of fear or unrealistic expectations, it's often too difficult for us to trust others with our hurts and disappointments. This Get-Together will help people be themselves, brokenness and all. They'll feel safe trusting others with their honest thoughts and feelings, and they'll dig deeper in a loving, healing friendship with God and others.

Get-Together at a Glance

	WHAT PEOPLE WILL DO	MINUTES	SUPPLIES
CAFÉ TIME	Eat a snack or meal that connects with today's point. OPTIONS (Choose One): ☐ *Quick and Easy:* Peanut Brittle ☐ *Easy Plus:* "Broken Glass" Dessert ☐ *High Impact:* Crunchy Chicken Salad	 10 to 15 30 60	See pp. 177-178 for details
EXPERIENCING FRIENDSHIP	*Broken Pieces* Share visible scar stories, and talk about other kinds of hurts people experience.	10 to 12	• *Friendship First* book for each person
	Rip It Up Do an active experience and talk more deeply about ways we hurt others and ways God heals.	10 to 12	• 1 person shape cut from paper per 6 people • 1 transparent-tape dispenser per 6 people • Bible
	The Invisibles Share invisible hurts and scars with partners and pray for each other.	10 to 12	• Bible • wrapped Band-Aids (1 per person) • pens
PRAYER	Symbolically pour water over each other's hands, and pray for God's healing and comfort in their brokenness.	5 to 10	• warm water (1 gallon per 3 to 4 people) • buckets or large bowls (2 for every 3 to 4 people) • towels (1 per 3 or 4 people) • *Friendship First* CD • CD player
DAILY CHALLENGE	Talk about the Daily Challenges they'll carry out during the week.	up to 5	• *Friendship First* book for each person

Café Time

What friendship doesn't include eating together? Food is a very important part of the Friendship First experience. As we eat together, we grow closer together—we relax, we smile, we share. It's the perfect beginning to each friendship Get-Together. Remember that during these Get-Togethers, your focus is on people. Take the time to enjoy the fellowship of the table together.

We've provided three delicious options for each week's Get-Together. Choose the one that best fits your time, your setting, and your budget. See pages 177-178 for details on today's menu options.

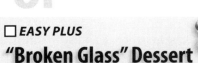

PURPOSE

Food that is broken will lead to discussion on our brokenness and God's unconditional love.

☐ **QUICK AND EASY**
Peanut Brittle

or

☐ **EASY PLUS**
"Broken Glass" Dessert

or

☐ **HIGH IMPACT**
Crunchy Chicken Salad

Music IDEAS

Set a great atmosphere by playing background music that matches the mood of this Get-Together! Here are some genre suggestions:

- piano or instrumental
- folk
- rock
- alternative

You can also play the *Friendship First* theme song, "Here for You" (track 11 on the *Friendship First* CD).

HERE'S WHAT TO DO

- Make sure that each person feels welcome and at home at today's Get-Together. You may personally welcome each person, or if you'll be busy getting the last-minute details organized, find a warm, friendly person to be the greeter.

- If you're using the **Quick and Easy** or **Easy Plus** option, invite people to get a snack before they sit down in their groups of six.

- If you're using the **High Impact** option, wait until everyone has arrived, and ask the blessing.

- Have everyone fill a plate, sit down, and begin eating.

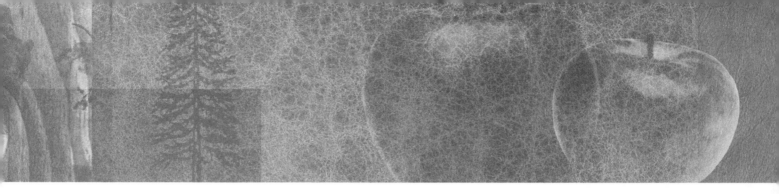

- While everyone's eating, allow for small talk and casual chatting.

- At some point in the conversation, continue discussing Chapter 4 in *Friendship First*. Ask people what struck them most from what they read.

- After a few minutes of discussion (or when there's a natural break in the conversation), discuss the significance of the food.

> **ASK** Let's brainstorm about all the ways this food might connect to friendship. How many can you think of?

> **SAY** Thanks for all your ideas! Today we're going to talk about brokenness. We'll discuss some of our hurts and failures and explore what it means to be broken yet loved completely. First let's check in on the Daily Challenges. How did you follow through with your Daily Challenge commitment, and what happened as a result?

- Give everyone an opportunity to share a Daily Challenge story.

- Thank everyone for sharing Daily Challenge stories.

INSIDE SCOOP During this discussion on Daily Challenges, we asked our group members why they do the Daily Challenges. Is it because they feel guilty or embarrassed if they don't complete the challenges? They responded unanimously that they were motivated by how meaningful the challenges are and how much they liked carrying them out. So encourage your group members to see how simple yet meaningful the Daily Challenge choices are. We guarantee they'll be "into" them!

Friendship First™ Gathering Cards and Nature Cards are a great way to show love and concern for the people in your group. Order at www.friendshipfirst.com.

EXPERIENCING Friendship

Broken Pieces

Do this activity to get people talking about their outward hurts.

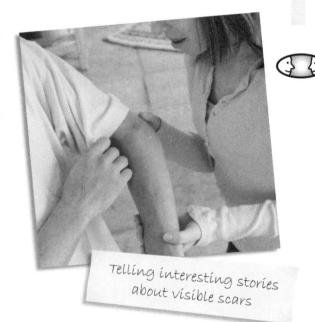

Telling interesting stories about visible scars

HERE'S WHAT TO DO

- Have people form pairs.

  SAY **Today we'll be talking about some of our deeper hurts. But let's start by telling each other about a visible scar we have and sharing the story behind it.**

- Expect pairs to have fun with these stories.

- After all pairs have shared visible-scar stories, get together as a group.

- Ask everyone to turn to page 39 in the *Friendship First* book and find the picture of the cracked clay pot.

- Encourage everyone to think of the pieces of a person's life that represent imperfections and brokenness. Have people write a different hurt on each piece of clay.

- Discuss these questions:

  ASK **What are different ways we experience hurt?**

  How do you think we might experience God's presence in these hurts?

Rip It Up

Do this activity as a powerful exploration of how people can hurt each other and contribute to each other's brokenness.

People rip a paper person while saying hurtful things.

HERE'S WHAT TO DO

- Before the Get-Together, cut one person shape from paper for every group of six people.

- Give each group a paper person.

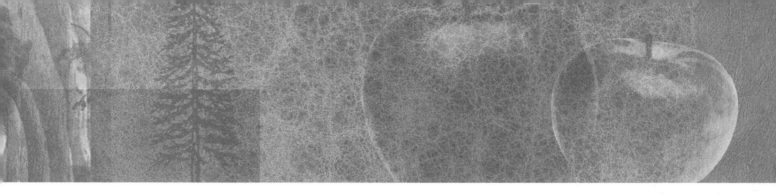

- As the leader, go first. Say "You're so stupid!" and rip off a piece of the paper person. (This will demonstrate what to do and will cause a surprised reaction.) Then pass the paper person to someone next to you.

- Whoever receives the paper person should say—in a word or phrase—a hurtful thing that people say or do to one another, tear a piece from the paper person, and hand the torn paper person to someone else.

- Have group members pass the paper person until you say "stop." (You may want the paper person to go around the group more than once.)

- Next, read aloud Ephesians 4:29:

  "Don't use foul or abusive language. Let everything you say be good and helpful, so that your words will be an encouragement to those who hear them."

- Give a tape dispenser to the group member holding the ripped paper person. Ask him or her to mention a kind thing that people can say or do to one another and use the tape to repair one rip in the paper person. That group member should then pass the paper person to the next group member, who will do the same thing.

- Continue until the paper person is intact, or call time.

- As a group, compare the taped person to its original appearance.

- Again, read aloud:

  "Don't use foul or abusive language. Let everything you say be good and helpful, so that your words will be an encouragement to those who hear them" (Ephesians 4:29).

Between Friends

It might be very difficult for people to say something deliberately hurtful. Use this emotional reaction to connect the activity to real life!

INSIDE SCOOP

We tested the paper-person activity with a wide range of people—new Christians, people hurt by church, people involved in church all their lives, people questioning their relationship with Jesus—and they all opened up more than ever while being very affected by the activity. View it as an "equalizing" experience, fitting all backgrounds and spiritual levels in your group.

Putting the paper person back together while sharing "healing" words

Between Friends

Sometimes it's impossible to put the paper person back together, so don't make this your goal. The purpose of the activity is that people find meaning in the taping process—whether it is completed or not.

However, people may be really intent on taping the person back together perfectly because they don't want it to be a sloppy "fix"—which would provide a good opportunity for further discussion. Ask, "How is this like how God views and treats us?"

ASK What were you feeling during this experience?

How were these feelings like or unlike what you've experienced in real life, particularly in friendships?

How has God "taped you up" where others have "ripped" you?

How is finding comfort through others like finding comfort in God?

FOR DEEPER IMPACT

You can explore Romans 8:28 in addition to Ephesians 4:29 while debriefing this paper-person activity. This verse provides insight into how God can work everything (even the most painful things) together for the best. What a great opportunity to talk about how God loves us and "tapes us together!"

3 The Invisibles

In this Band-Aid activity, people will dig a little deeper into the pain of brokenness, identify specific emotional or spiritual scars, and encourage each other toward healing.

HERE'S WHAT TO DO

SAY We've talked about our visible scars and about the power we hold to tear down or build each other up. Now let's talk about invisible scars.

- Have everyone find a partner, and have partners share invisible scars with each other.

- After everyone has shared an invisible scar and the story that goes along with it, have pairs discuss these questions:

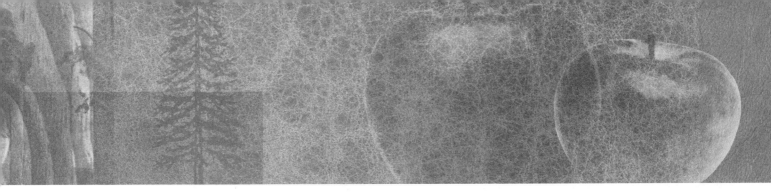

ASK What did you discover during this experience about your invisible hurts and scars?

What does it mean to you that Jesus understands your brokenness and still loves you?

How might we understand our friends' brokenness and love them the way Jesus loves them?

- Give everyone a wrapped Band-Aid and a pen.

- Have people write their own name on the Band-Aid and exchange Band-Aids with their partners.

- Have pairs take a minute or two to pray silently that Jesus will heal their partners' invisible hurts and scars.

SAY This Band-Aid will be a reminder for you to pray for your partner. Keep it in your purse, bag, or wallet as a reminder. (Smile.) And it's always good to have a Band-Aid—just in case!

- Have people gather as a group.

- Have a volunteer read Romans 5:6-11 aloud:

"**When we were utterly helpless, Christ came at just the right time and died for us sinners. Now, most people would not be willing to die for an upright person, though someone might perhaps be willing to die for a person who is especially good. But God showed his great love for us by sending Christ to die for us while we were still sinners. And since we have been made right in God's sight by the blood of Christ, he will certainly save us from God's judgment. For since our friendship with God was restored by the death of his Son while we were still his enemies, we will certainly be saved through the life of his Son. So now we can rejoice in our wonderful new relationship with God because our Lord Jesus Christ has made us friends of God.**"

Between Friends

If people struggle with identifying invisible scars, tell them to think of anything that caused them to feel hurt, ashamed, or a sense of failure. The invisible scar could be something specific, such as a relationship problem or a work, school, or church situation. Or it could be a general area of struggle, such as trust, acceptance, or making friends. Emphasize that the purpose of this activity is not to feel discouraged or wallow in hurts. Instead, sharing pain and brokenness with a friend helps open the door to Jesus' healing and unconditional love.

· ·

As you discuss the hurts, shame, and failures of life, be aware that some people may not have realized—or be willing to admit—that they are broken. Spend a few minutes exploring 1 John 1:8-9 aloud, and discuss what truths this passage teaches about our brokenness. Allow people to discover or face the brokenness, hurts, and failures they may have been avoiding their entire lives.

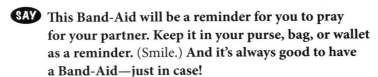

Partners exchange Band-Aids so they can pray for each other's healing.

*Find comfort
in Jesus
and others.*

Receiving God's unconditional
love and healing through a
water pouring prayer

INSIDE SCOOP After a sometimes painful and serious time, this was a comforting and healing way to end the Get-Together; the youth in our group really got into the praying and water pouring. Also, the water represented different things to different teenagers— God's grace washing away sin, God healing hurts, God taking away hurts we don't hold on to anymore. Encourage everyone to consider and pray about the many different connections.

Prayer

Go through this prayer experience in a quiet and reflective mood.

HERE'S WHAT TO DO

• Form smaller groups of three to five people. Have the small groups separate themselves around the room.

• Make sure each group has a full bucket (or large bowl), an empty bucket, and a towel.

• Hold up a bucket filled with one gallon of water.

SAY **This prayer experience might be very different from anything you've done before. It might be a little beyond your comfort zone, but let's give this a try. Imagine that this bucket represents your brokenness—it contains all of your scars, hurts, shames, and failures. Each of you will take turns doing the prayer activity in your group. You should hold your hands over the empty bucket while one of your friends pours the water into your hands. You will try to grasp as much of the water as you can, presenting your hurts to God. Let this be a time of honesty before God, as you accept that Jesus understands your brokenness and loves you completely.**

• Play "Who Am I" (track 5) on the *Friendship First* CD while the group is pouring the water into each other's hands.

• The "pour-er" should slowly pour the whole bucket of water into the person's hands.

• The "pray-er" should pray (either aloud or silently) as the water drips through his or her hands, talking to God about being broken, understood, and loved.

• Others in the group should affirm the "pray-er" by gently placing hands on the "pray-er's" shoulders, smiling warmly, or saying something encouraging after the prayer.

• Make sure each person in every small group gets a turn to pour and a turn to pray.

• Allow four or five minutes for this activity. Even though this is a contemplative, prayerful activity, expect some laughter and maybe a few spills—that's what the towels are for!

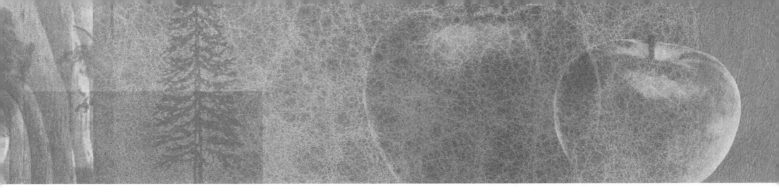

- Close with a prayer.

PRAY **Jesus, we know that we've been hurt and we've hurt others. You are the God of restoration, repair, and healing. Thank you for dying on the cross so that your grace can wash away our sins. We accept your healing, and ask you to forgive us where we've hurt others. Amen.**

Daily Challenge™

The Daily Challenges will give people an opportunity to practice what they explored during the week's Get-Together.

HERE'S WHAT TO DO

- Have everyone go to page 132 of the *Friendship First* book. Have a volunteer read the "Find Comfort" Daily Challenges aloud.

- Have everyone choose one of the challenges to do in the coming week and mark it in his or her book. Ask people to take turns around the room telling which challenge they plan to do.

- Have people take home their Band-Aids, which symbolize their commitments to find comfort in Jesus and others. The Band-Aids will be tangible reminders to follow through on the Daily Challenge.

- Tell everyone to be ready to report how the Daily Challenge went next time the group meets.

- Encourage everyone to continue reading Chapter 4 of *Friendship First* book throughout the week.

6. Find Comfort
in Jesus and Others

☐ Avoid criticizing or correcting someone unnecessarily. Instead offer kind words and build up the person with encouragement. Notice what happens between the two of you.

☐ Describe an emotional scar, or tell a story of your own brokenness to someone this week. Tell how God has healed (or is healing) you.

☐ Tuck your Friendship First partner's Band-Aid in your purse or wallet, and each time you reach inside, pray for your partner. Or think of a friend who has helped heal your hurts, and write his or her name on a Band-Aid.

☐ Find your favorite, most comfortable place to relax, and focus on Jesus' love. Breathe slowly and deeply. Let the words from Romans 8:35-39 comfort you.

GET-TOGETHER

7

Trust your true self to Jesus and others.

PSALM 139:1-6

It's been said that the best friends are the ones who know all about us but love us anyway. That's certainly true about our Best Friend. Even so, it's tough to trust Jesus with our true selves. We naturally try to hide the things we're ashamed of. We try to cover up our insecurities because that's what we do in our earthly friendships. If people knew the real us, we reason, they'd reject us or ridicule us or, at the very least, think less of us.

But that's not a risk we face with Jesus. He already knows the good and the bad. And through his forgiveness, our sinful imperfections disappear. Jesus offers us complete acceptance. We can stand completely open before our friend Jesus and find the kind of true intimate friendship that only comes from complete honesty. In response, we can follow the example of our Best Friend and offer acceptance and intimate friendship to others.

Get-Together at a Glance

	WHAT PEOPLE WILL DO	MINUTES	SUPPLIES
CAFÉ TIME	Eat a snack or meal that connects with today's point. OPTIONS (Choose One): ☐ *Quick and Easy:* Filled Doughnuts ☐ *Easy Plus:* Hidden Snacks ☐ *High Impact:* Variety of Burritos	10 to 15 30 60	See pp. 179-180 for details
EXPERIENCING FRIENDSHIP	*Friendly Revelations* Tell partners things about themselves that partners don't know.	10 to 12	
	Ogres and Onions Watch a clip from *Shrek* and talk about their hidden layers.	10 to 12	• *Shrek* DVD • DVD player and TV • *Friendship First* book per person • pens
	Sharing Ourselves Explore what it means to be transparent.	10 to 12	• 2 sealed packets of Alka-Seltzer and large jar of water per group of 6 to 8
	Trustworthy Explore what it means to be trustworthy in friendships.	10 to 12	• *Friendship First* book per person • Bible
PRAYER	Pray about trusting God with themselves.	5 to 10	• *Friendship First* CD • CD player • Bible
DAILY CHALLENGE	Talk about the Daily Challenges they'll carry out during the week.	up to 5	• *Friendship First* book per person • pens • 1 onion per person

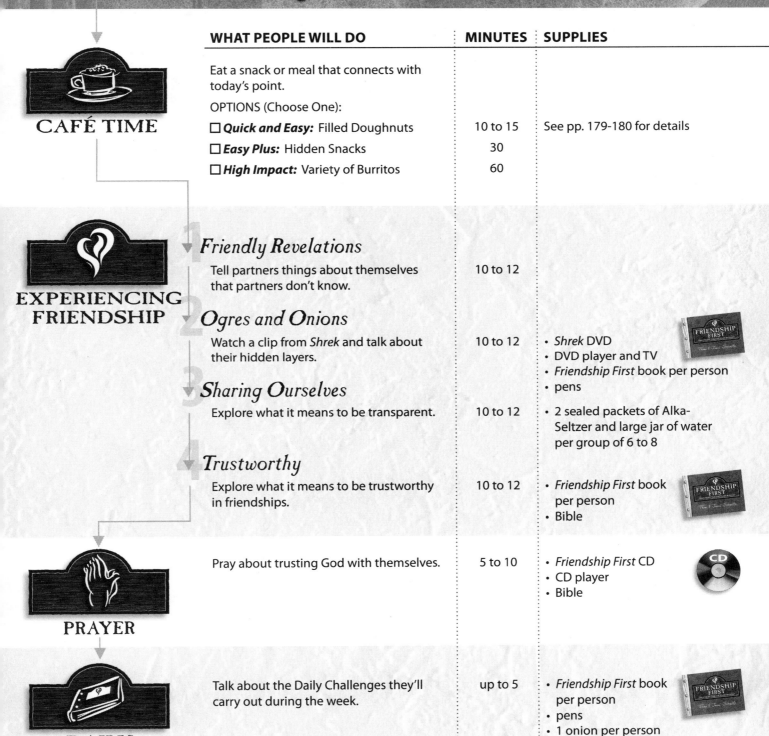

Trust your true self to Jesus and others.

What friendship doesn't include eating together? Food is a very important part of the Friendship First experience. As we eat together, we grow closer together—we relax, we smile, we share. It's the perfect beginning to each friendship Get-Together. Remember that during these Get-Togethers, your focus is on people. Take the time to enjoy the fellowship of the table together.

We've provided three delicious options for each week's Get-Together. Choose the one that best fits your time, your setting, and your budget. See pages 179-180 for details on today's menu options.

Music IDEAS

Set a great atmosphere by playing background music that matches the mood of this Get-Together! Here are some genre suggestions:

- mariachi
- salsa
- Latin
- pop

You can also play the *Friendship First* theme song, "Here for You" (track 11 on the *Friendship First* CD).

Café Time

PURPOSE

Today's Get-Together is about being transparent before Jesus and others. It's about trusting others enough to reveal our hidden selves. In each of today's options, there's something hidden that will be revealed when participants dig in to the food.

☐ **QUICK AND EASY**
Filled Doughnuts

or

☐ **EASY PLUS**
Hidden Snacks

or

☐ **HIGH IMPACT**
Variety of Burritos

HERE'S WHAT TO DO

- Make sure that each person feels welcome and at home at today's Get-Together. You may personally welcome each person, or if you'll be busy getting the last-minute details organized, find a warm, friendly person to be the greeter.

- If you're using the **Quick and Easy** or **Easy Plus** option, invite people to get a snack before they sit down in their groups of six.

- If you're using the **High Impact** option, wait until everyone has arrived.

- Ask the blessing.

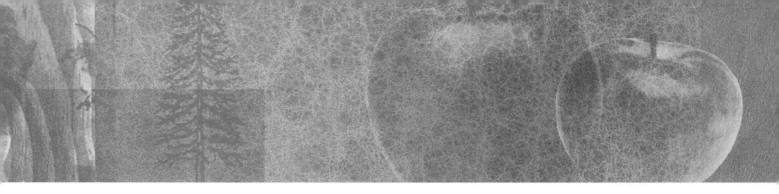

- Have everyone fill a plate, sit down, and begin eating.

- While everyone's eating, encourage small talk and casual chatting.

- At some point in the conversation, discuss Chapter 4 in *Friendship First*. Ask people what struck them most about what they read.

- After a few minutes of discussion (or when there's a natural break in the conversation), discuss the significance of the food.

ASK **What could the food we're eating today symbolize about friendship? Let's think of as many possibilities as we can.**

SAY **These are all great insights into friendship. Today we'll be talking about trust and being transparent and open with others. Today's food has several different kinds of fillings. You didn't know what you'd get until you started eating. People often don't reveal all of themselves to others. It's not until we trust each other as good friends that we discover some of these hidden things about each other. Today we'll talk about the role trust plays in being open with each other.**

SAY **Now let's check in on our Daily Challenges. How did you follow through with your Daily Challenge commitment? What happened as a result?**

- Thank everyone for sharing a Daily Challenge story.

EXPERIENCING Friendship

Friendly Revelations

This fun activity will help group members get to know each other better.

HERE'S WHAT TO DO

- Have everyone find a partner.

- Have people tell their partner at least three things that the partner doesn't know about them. For example, maybe a partner doesn't know that the other partner hiked three-fourths of the Appalachian Trail or once parachuted out of an airplane. Make sure everyone understands that these things will be shared with the rest of the group.

- When both partners have had a chance to share, have each person tell the rest of the group what he or she discovered.

- Then discuss these questions:

  ASK **How does it feel to tell others things they don't know about us?**

  How does it feel to be trusted with intimate details of others' lives?

Ogres and Onions

You'll need a DVD of *Shrek* for this activity. Cue the DVD to Scene 6.

This fun media activity will help the members of your group explore how comfortable they feel about revealing their inner selves to others.

HERE'S WHAT TO DO

 SAY **Shrek is a movie about an ogre who lives in a swamp. Shrek is a loner—he's a little different from most folks and has had some trouble being accepted. He has**

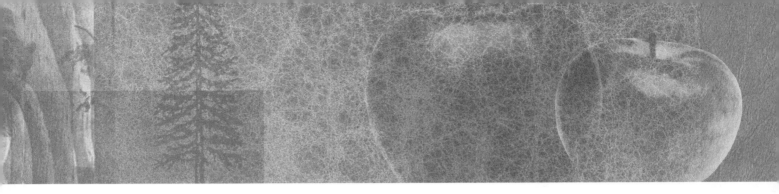

decided that it's much easier to live alone than to risk the disapproval he has encountered in the past. At the beginning of the movie, he encounters a donkey who insists on being his friend and companion on a noble quest. Let's see what Shrek has to say.

• Show the movie clip. Turn off the DVD as soon as Shrek says, "Bye-bye. See you later." There's a bit of mild profanity in the next sentence.

• Discuss these questions:

ASK What did Shrek mean when he said he had "layers"?

Why are ogres and people reluctant to share their layers with others?

Have everyone turn to page 50 in their *Friendship First* books. Have someone in the group read aloud the section titled "Like an Onion."

Have each person work independently to write his or her "layers" below the onion illustration in the book.

Like an Onion

Another way to think about transparency is to consider an onion. How are you like an onion? What are the layers that contribute to your composition as a person? What layers do most people see on first observation? What parts are buried in the deeper layers that you allow few or no one to see?

Respect confidentiality. Trust implies safety. It means friends can rely on one another to keep confidential matters confidential. Few things destroy trust faster than a loose-lipped friend.

We've known Marsha (not her real name) for many years. She's a fun, creative, caring person. In fact, she's typically the first person to respond to anyone's crisis. She won our trust early in the relationship. We began to share with her some hurts and struggles. Then we learned she shared that information with others outside our circle of friends. That brought our trust to a swift end.

We noticed that Marsha often shared juicy information about other people. (She knows everybody!)

50

• Have people turn to a partner and talk about their layers.

• Discuss these questions in small groups:

ASK How did you feel as you shared the layers of who you are with someone else?

What risks and rewards come with sharing who we really are?

SAY Find your partners, and affirm them by mentioning one thing you really like about who they are and what they revealed to you about themselves.

• Give pairs time to do this.

GET-TOGETHER

7

*Trust your
true self to
Jesus and others.*

Plop, plop! Fizz, fizz! This demonstration leads to discoveries about being open with others.

Sharing Ourselves

This activity will help people realize that sharing themselves with others is risky but almost always pays off. For each group of six to eight, you'll need two sealed packets of Alka-Seltzer and a large jar of water.

HERE'S WHAT TO DO

 Let's explore this idea of being transparent with others. This demonstration will give us lots of insights into revealing our inner selves to others.

- Unwrap one Alka-Seltzer packet. Drop the tablet into the water. Drop the other still-sealed Alka-Seltzer packet into the water.

- Have everyone watch the Alka-Seltzer tablets for about a minute.

- Discuss these questions:

 What insights about being open and transparent with others can you glean from this demonstration? Let's come up with as many insights as we can.

What happens in our relationships when we're open and transparent with others? If possible, tell a story from your own experience.

Trustworthy

This activity will help people explore how to build trust so they can be transparent in their relationships with others and God.

HERE'S WHAT TO DO

- Have everyone turn to page 44 in the *Friendship First* book. Have one person in each group read the "Aged to Perfection" section of Chapter 4 aloud. The reader should stop at the heading "Building Trust."

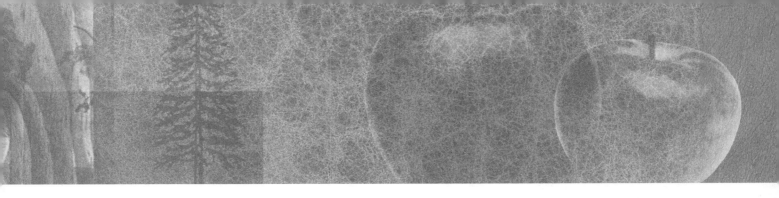

 • Have everyone turn to a partner. Ask partners to share about a time trust between them and a friend was either built or broken.

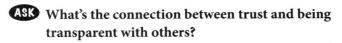 • Have the group come back together. Discuss these questions:

ASK **What's the connection between trust and being transparent with others?**

How do we build trust in our friendships?

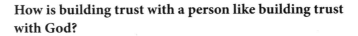 **How is building trust with a person like building trust with God?**

• Read John 12:44, 46:

"Jesus shouted to the crowds, 'If you trust me, you are trusting not only me, but also God who sent me. I have come as a light to shine in this dark world, so that all who put their trust in me will no longer remain in the dark."

 • Discuss these questions:

ASK **Why is trusting God important?**

What role does trusting God play in coming out of the dark?

 • You may want to end this activity by having everyone listen to the *Friendship First* theme song, "Here for You" (track 11 on the *Friendship First* CD).

GET-TOGETHER

7

*Trust your
true self to
Jesus and others.*

Prayer

This prayer activity will help people pray about trusting God with their own fragile selves.

HERE'S WHAT TO DO

- Play "Prayer Music," track 6 of the *Friendship First* CD.

  SAY **In just a moment, you'll have a chance to talk to God. To begin our prayer, I'd like to read several verses of Scripture. Make these verses your prayer too.**

- Have each person stand a little apart from everyone else in the group. Have people hold their palms face up and lift their faces to heaven, in a posture of openness before God.

- Read Psalm 139:1-6 aloud:

  "O Lord, you have examined my heart and know everything about me. You know when I sit down or stand up. You know my thoughts even when I'm far away. You see me when I travel and when I rest at home. You know everything I do. You know what I am going to say even before I say it, Lord. You go before me and follow me. You place your hand of blessing on my head. Such knowledge is too wonderful for me, too great for me to understand!"

- Ask everyone to continue to stand with eyes closed and hands outstretched.

  SAY **We are already transparent before God—there is nothing hidden. There's one question, though, that remains. Do you trust God with this knowledge of yourself? Will you stand before him as you are, trusting him to treat you with gentle friendship and love? Or will you try to hide yourself from him or close yourself off from him?**

- Invite the group to pray silently. When the music ends, close the Get-Together with a prayer, asking God to help you all trust God with your true selves.

A posture of openness helps participants be transparent before God during prayer.

INSIDE SCOOP People were a bit self-conscious about adopting this posture at first. But soon they turned their attention to God and their self-consciousness melted away. How we hold ourselves physically can affect our attitude and emotions, so encourage everyone to be open to God in both attitude and stance.

Daily Challenge™

The Daily Challenge will give people an opportunity to practice what they explored during the week's Get-Together.

HERE'S WHAT TO DO

- Have everyone turn to page 133 in the *Friendship First* book. Have a volunteer read the "Trust Our True Selves" Daily Challenges aloud.

- Have everyone choose one of the challenges to do in the coming week and mark it in the book. Have people take turns around the room telling which challenge they plan to do.

- Give everyone a small onion as a reminder to open up and show his or her "layers" to God and others by doing the Daily Challenge.

- Tell everyone to be ready to report how the Daily Challenge went next time you meet.

- Encourage everyone to continue reading Chapter 4 of *Friendship First* during the week.

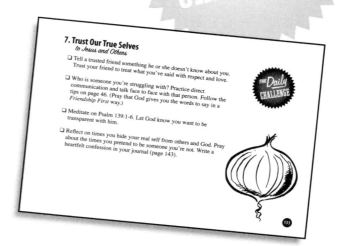

7. Trust Our True Selves
to Jesus and Others

❑ Tell a trusted friend something he or she doesn't know about you. Trust your friend to treat what you've said with respect and love.

❑ Who is someone you're struggling with? Practice direct communication and talk face to face with that person. Follow the tips on page 46. (Pray that God gives you the words to say in a *Friendship First* way.)

❑ Meditate on Psalm 139:1-6. Let God know you want to be transparent with him.

❑ Reflect on times you hide your real self from others and God. Pray about the times you pretend to be someone you're not. Write a heartfelt confession in your journal (page 143).

GET-TOGETHER

8

Experience forgiveness through Jesus and others.

COLOSSIANS 3:13

Choosing to forgive is tough—especially when we struggle with anger, hurt, and resentment against people who have hurt us. Receiving forgiveness can be even tougher—especially from a close friend. And accepting forgiveness from God may be the most difficult of all. Help the people in your group discover how forgiveness can free them from guilt and pain, as well as deepen their friendships in amazing ways. Through the powerful stations in this Get-Together, they will experience Jesus' transforming forgiveness!

Get-Together at a Glance

	WHAT PEOPLE WILL DO	MINUTES	SUPPLIES
 **CAFÉ TIME**	Eat a snack or meal that connects with today's point. OPTIONS *(Choose One):* ☐ ***Quick and Easy:*** Biscotti and Hot Chocolate ☐ ***Easy Plus:*** Baked Brie ☐ ***High Impact:*** Build-Your-Own French Onion Soup	10 to 15 30 60	See pp. 181-182 for details
 **EXPERIENCING FRIENDSHIP**	*Simple Seal* Watch a video segment about forgiveness, share personal stories, and respond to the message of Jesus' forgiveness. *Jesus' Passion Stations* Travel through experiential stations at which they will discover and respond to Jesus' transforming forgiveness.	10 to 12 10 to 12	• *Friendship First* DVD • *Friendship First* book for each person • *Friendship First* book for each person • pens or pencils • *Friendship First* CD (See station supplies and setup details, pp. 92-96)
 **PRAYER**	Pray about and commit to sharing Jesus' forgiveness with others.	5 to 10	(See station supplies and setup details, pp. 92-96)
 **DAILY CHALLENGE**	Talk about the Daily Challenges they'll carry out during the week.	up to 5	• *Friendship First* book for each person

Before the Get-Together

Follow the instructions below to set up for "Jesus' Passion Stations." Adjust the supplies and amounts for your group.

STATION 1

- 2 or 3 objects with sharp points, such as a needle, pin, thistle, or thorn (You might bring in a rose that still has its thorns.)

- photocopy of "The Painful Thorns" (p. 107)

- tape

Setup: Tape the copy of "The Painful Thorns" instructions to a wall or other surface, or attach it to a piece of cardboard and prop it up at the station. Lay the objects on a table or even on the floor so participants may pick them up and hold them.

If you want to go all out, make barbed-wire crowns by shaping 10-inch lengths of barbed wire into circles. Try a local fencing company for the barbed wire. You'll also need a wire cutter. Use duct tape to bind together the ends of each barbed wire circle. It's OK if the ends don't meet perfectly.

STATION 2

- one or two pieces of scrap wood thick enough that nails won't go all the through them (Two 2x4s put together, scraps from a lumber store, or firewood from the grocery story would work.)

- 6 to 8 nails, size 60d

- 3 or 4 medium-size hammers

- floor mat, pieces of fabric, or carpet (if the floor isn't carpeted)

- photocopy of "The Spike of Sin" (p. 108)

- tape

Setup: Tape "The Spike of Sin" copy to a wall or other surface, or attach it to a piece of cardboard and prop it up at the station. It's best if the floor is carpeted. If the floor is not carpeted, lay the fabric, mat,

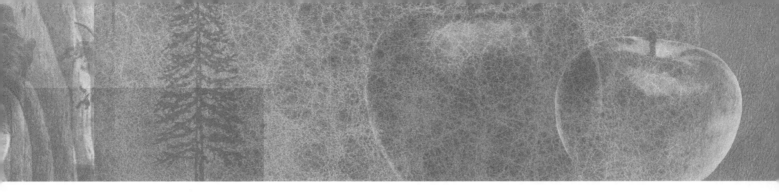

or carpet under the wood to protect the floor and reduce the bounce when participants strike the nails. Space the nails 1 foot apart, and pound them into the wood just enough to secure them. Leave the spikes sticking up so participants can strike them with a hammer. Then set the pieces of wood, nails up, on the mat or floor. Place hammers around the wood for participants to use.

If you want to go all out, position the pieces of wood in the shape of a cross. Use nails, rope, or duct tape to secure the pieces in place.

Safety issue: You might wish to be available at this station to step in if participants become too aggressive with the hammers or otherwise act in unsafe ways. You might also want to use wood spacers to raise the wood pieces a little higher off the floor to prevent the spikes from going into the floor.

STATION 3

- 2 bowls (plastic, disposable, cereal-size will work fine)

- 1 bottle of cider vinegar

- cotton-tipped swabs for all participants

- wastebasket

- tablecloth

- photocopy of "The Bitter Vinegar" (p. 109)

- tape

Setup: Tape "The Bitter Vinegar" sign to a wall or other surface, or attach it to a piece of cardboard and prop it up at the station. Spread a tablecloth over the table or area (for spills). Place the bowls at either end of the table. Pour the cider vinegar in the bowls. Spread the cotton swabs evenly around each bowl. Place the wastebasket beside the table so participants may discard their cotton swabs after they use them.

STATION 4

- 4 or 5 dice (Packs of dice can be found in the games and toys section of department stores.)

- white sheet (Twin size is fine. A white tablecloth would also work.)

- chair

- photocopy of "Distracting Dice" (p. 110)

- tape

Setup: Tape the "Distracting Dice" copy to a wall or other surface, or attach it to a piece of cardboard and prop it up at the station. Drape the white sheet over the chair so part of the sheet is spread on the floor. The sheet is to remind people of Jesus' robe. Set the dice on the floor on top of the sheet.

STATION 5

- sheet of newsprint, 5x10 feet

- 4 to 6 red markers

- permanent black marker

- photocopy of "Remember Me" (p. 111)

- tape

Setup: Tape the "Remember Me" copy to a wall or other surface, or attach it to a piece of cardboard and prop it up at the station. Tape the newsprint to the wall. Using the black marker, write "REMEMBER ME" in large letters at the center top of the paper. Set the red markers on the floor beneath the newsprint.

If you want to go all out, get red tempera paint, which you can find at craft supply stores, and three or four disposable aluminum pie pans so that participants can dip their fingers into the paint to write their names. Spread black tarp or other protective material on the floor beneath the sign and, if you think it might be needed, on the wall behind the sign. Pour the tempera paint into pie pans, and set the pans on the tarp. Place many paper towels between each pie pan.

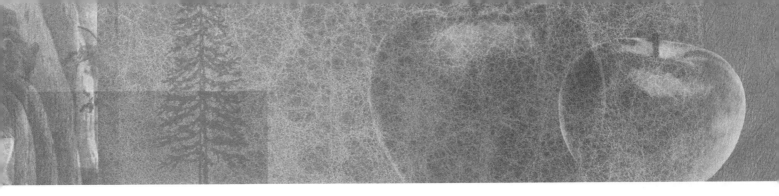

Place a wastebasket beside the wall so participants can discard paper towels in it.

Tempera paint is made from eggs and will wash off surfaces easily. Nevertheless, you'll want to clean it up quickly afterwards. Any spots you miss will chip off very easily when dry.

A few minutes before the activity, have someone pour half an inch of paint into each pan. (If you pour the paint too early, the paint will dry.)

STATION 6

- 1 large piece of cotton material (such as an old sheet or pillowcase)

- scissors

- photocopy of "The New Agreement With God" (p. 112)

- tape

Setup: Tape "The New Agreement With God" copy to a wall or other surface, or attach it to a piece of cardboard and prop it up at the station. Cut many little slits in the material to make ripping easier, then set the piece of material at the station with the pair of scissors.

If you want to go all out, cut one 4- or 6-inch square of lightweight, solid-color (such as light tan or beige) fabric for every person. Snip a 1-inch cut in each fabric piece so it can be easily torn. The sections need not be the same size. In fact, it's more interesting when they're different sizes. But keep them close to the 4- to 6-inch range.

GET-TOGETHER

8

*Experience
forgiveness through
Jesus and others.*

STATION 7

- large pillar candle of any kind

- candleholder for pillar candle

- 1 small candle (tea-light candle, for example) for each person

- basket or other container to hold the small candles

- vinyl tablecloth or several trash bags

- matches or lighter

Setup: Spread the tablecloth or bags over the area to protect it from wax drippings. Place the candleholder in the center. Next to it place the basket filled with the small candles. The large pillar candle and the lighter will be near the presenter, who will eventually light the candle and set it on the candleholder.

Note: It's best to light the pillar candle before the activity and let it burn for a minute or two. Also, if the candleholder has a sharp spike to hold the candle, place the candle on the holder beforehand to "predrill" the hole.

Safety Issue: It's very important that the lit candles are never left unattended. Make sure a couple of attendants are standing by to keep an eye on this station for safety. Having a fire extinguisher on hand is a must. The pillar candle has a tendency to go out as participants surround it, so be ready to relight it (and some of the smaller candles) as necessary.

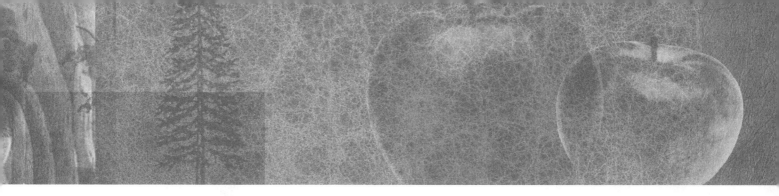

SETUP POINTERS

The "Jesus Passion Stations" provide a powerful experience of Jesus' love and forgiveness. To maximize the experience and keep distractions to a minimum, we recommend the following:

- Set up the stations so they're sufficiently apart from one another. Expect some clumping as people gather at each station, and provide plenty of room so that participants can move around freely.

- The fewer obstacles in the room, the better. This experience works best in a flat, open space, such as a fellowship hall or large room. People will need to move freely around to make the experience effective.

- Spend time to achieve the right lighting for the space. The room should be fairly dim so that people get the full effect of the candles at the last station. Semidarkness will also help participants focus on worship and prayer. At the same time, people need to be able to see the other stations and read the signs. You may want to cover up windows with blinds or black plastic.

- Be prepared to pray with or counsel participants after they experience these stations.

INSIDE SCOOP We found that this Get-Together requires more supplies and preparation than some of the others. But don't miss out on this powerful experience. Combine all your resources, enlist helpers, and start early! The result will be more than worth your efforts.

GET-TOGETHER

8

Experience forgiveness through Jesus and others.

Café Time

What friendship doesn't include eating together? Food is a very important part of the Friendship First experience. As we eat together, we grow closer together—we relax, we smile, we share. It's the perfect beginning to each friendship Get-Together. Remember that during these Get-Togethers, your focus is on people. Take the time to enjoy the fellowship of the table together.

We've provided three delicious options for each week's Get-Together. Choose the one that best fits your time, your setting, and your budget. See pages 181-182 for details on today's menu options.

PURPOSE

Food that is hard and then softens will lead into discussion about how forgiveness softens us.

☐ *QUICK AND EASY*
Biscotti and Hot Chocolate

or

☐ *EASY PLUS*
Baked Brie

or

☐ *HIGH IMPACT*
French Onion Soup

Music IDEAS

Set a great atmosphere by playing background music that matches the mood of this Get-Together! Here are some genre suggestions:
- classical
- world
- electronic

You can also play the Friendship First theme song, "Here for You" (track 11 on the *Friendship First* CD).

HERE'S WHAT TO DO

- Make sure that each person feels welcome and at home at today's Get-Together. You may personally welcome each person, or if you'll be busy getting the last-minute details organized, find a warm, friendly person to be the greeter.

- If you're using the **Quick and Easy** or **Easy Plus** option, invite people to get a snack before they sit down in their groups of six.

- If you're using the **High Impact** option, wait until everyone has arrived, and ask the blessing.

- Have everyone fill a plate, sit down, and begin eating.

- While people eat, allow for small talk and casual chatting.

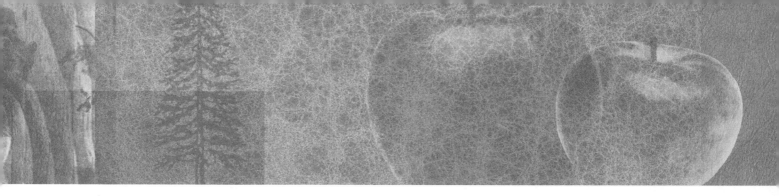

- While everyone's eating, allow for small talk and casual chatting.

- At some point in the conversation, discuss Chapter 5 in the *Friendship First* book. Ask people what struck them most.

- After a few minutes of discussion (or when there's a natural break in the conversation), discuss the significance of the food.

 ASK **What could the food we're eating today symbolize about friendship? Let's think of as many possibilities as we can.**

SAY **Thanks for all your ideas! We see how our food has been softened and changed; forgiveness has the power to soften and change us as people. Today we're going to talk about forgiveness. We'll discuss what it means to be forgiven and to forgive others, and we'll explore how Jesus' forgiveness changes us.**

 First let's check in on the Daily Challenges. How did you follow through with your Daily Challenge commitment? What happened as a result?

- Thank everyone for sharing a Daily Challenge story.

EXPERIENCING Friendship

Simple Seal

In this activity, people will share personal experiences of forgiveness and discover the life-changing power of Jesus' forgiveness.

HERE'S WHAT TO DO

> **SAY** **To start us off in our discussion, let's watch some scenes that deal with forgiveness.**

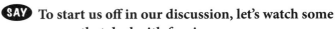

- Show the segment titled "Forgiveness" on the *Friendship First* DVD.

- Discuss these questions:

> **ASK** **What discoveries can we make about forgiveness?**
>
> **What effect does forgiveness have on us?**

- Have people form pairs to discuss:

> **ASK** **When have you experienced forgiveness? What was it like? (This could be a time you forgave someone or were forgiven.)**
>
> **Think of someone who was hard to forgive. Why was that person hard to forgive? (Remember not to reveal names.)**

- While people are still in pairs, read Colossians 3:13 aloud:

> **"Make allowance for each other's faults, and forgive anyone who offends you. Remember, the Lord forgave you, so you must forgive others."**

- Have partners discuss these questions:

> **ASK** **Why is forgiving others important to our friendship with Jesus?**
>
> **How can you forgive, even when it's hard?**
>
> **How is experiencing forgiveness from another person like experiencing forgiveness from God?**

- Have everyone go to page 81 of *Friendship First* and read the "Forgiveness" section together.

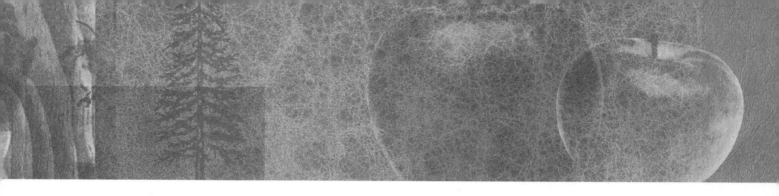

- Have everyone go to page 117 and read the box "A Simple Seal of Friendship" individually.

  SAY Consider how you want to respond to Jesus' love and forgiveness. Let's take a few quiet moments to talk privately to God. Pray this prayer if it is the true desire of your heart.

- After a minute or two,

  SAY Now we'll discover more about this greatest story of forgiveness and continue to respond to Jesus' love. We'll also search our own lives and hearts for how we can freely forgive others.

2 Jesus' Passion Stations

In this transforming experience, people will respond to Jesus' forgiveness and pray about their own forgiveness for others.

HERE'S WHAT TO DO

SAY Forgiveness is not saying that something that someone's done to hurt us is OK. It's letting go of our right to revenge and freeing that person from retaliation or punishment. Our sin is not OK, but Jesus has provided a way to free us from the punishment our sin deserves.

We'll understand Jesus' forgiveness even better by transporting ourselves to the foot of the cross and experiencing the passion of Jesus.

You'll find stations around the room to help you reconnect with Jesus' sacrifice and grace. You'll go through six of the stations on your own. You'll take your book with you and use the last few pages as a journal, writing your thoughts, feelings, and prayers about the experience. We'll do the seventh station together later.

First I'll take a few moments to explain how you'll experience the stations. There are also explanations

Thanking Jesus for taking on painful thorns in life

Asking God for forgiveness for sin

Praying that God will take away bitterness and replace it with sweetness

in your books and instructions at each station to help you.

- Turn off or dim the lights in the room to create a meditative atmosphere.

- Describe each of the first six stations by explaining the Scripture background of the activity and telling people what they'll do.

• Station 1: The Painful Thorns

Before his death, Jesus received a crown of thorns.

Participants will hold the object and run their thumbs over its point. As they feel the sharpness, they'll thank Jesus for enduring the pain on the cross and for taking on the thorns in their life. They'll also pray that God will take away the pain that they suffer from not forgiving others.

• Station 2: The Spike of Sin

The Roman soldiers hammered spikes into Jesus' hands and feet.

Participants will strike nails with a hammer and ask for forgiveness for a specific sin in their lives.

• Station 3: The Bitter Vinegar

While he hung on the cross, Jesus was offered a taste of vinegar for his thirst.

Participants will dip a cotton swab in the vinegar and reflect on bitter times in their lives. They'll pray that God will help them to forgive, give them a soft and sweet heart toward others, and remove their bitterness.

• Station 4: Distracting Dice

The soldiers gambled for Jesus' robe, ignoring the Son of God who hung nearby. John 19:24 says, "So they said, 'Rather than tearing it apart, Let's throw dice for it.' This fulfilled the Scripture that says, 'They divided my garments among themselves and threw dice for my clothing.' "

Participants will roll a single die. They'll look at the number that comes up and name that many of the distractions that keep them from experiencing Jesus' forgiveness. They'll pray that God will help them focus on Jesus instead.

• Station 5: Remember Me

One of the thieves crucified beside Jesus begged him to "Remember me" in heaven.

Participants will write their names in red under the words "REMEMBER ME" and thank Jesus for forgiving them and loving them eternally.

• Station 6: The New Agreement With God

The Temple once had a thick curtain that divided the Holy Place, where the people could go, from the Most Holy Place, where God was. When Jesus died, the curtain ripped from top to bottom. There was no more separation between God and us. When the army officer who was standing in front of the cross saw what had happened when Jesus died, he said, "This man truly was the Son of God!"

Participants will tear a piece of cloth and thank God for ripping through that barrier in their lives so that they can be friends with Jesus. You may want to tell them to start the cloth with scissors and then rip it.

After you've described the first six stations,

SAY This room is now a sanctuary. You will be free to experience as many or as few of these six stations as you like, in any order, but please don't do the seventh station, "Light of the World," yet. I'll let you know when we have five minutes left. The only thing I ask during this time is that you remain silent and go through these stations slowly and meditatively. You have a lot of time and space to experience them.

When you've finished the six stations, you may return to your seat and continue writing, thinking, and praying. This is a time for personal reflection and intimate time with God. You are now free to experience the Passion and the forgiveness that Jesus

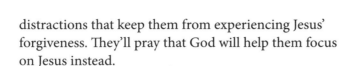
Reflecting on specific distractions in life, and praying for focus on Jesus

Thanking God for his love and forgiveness

Tearing cloth to symbolize how God tore down the barrier between us and Jesus

*Experience
forgiveness through
Jesus and others.*

Christ has for you. I pray God touches you deeply.

- Play track 7 on the *Friendship First* CD as people go through the stations.

- Allow plenty of time for people to go through the six stations. It's OK if some finish before others or if some spend most of their time at one station. How the participants experience these activities is entirely up to them.

- Let everyone know when there are five minutes left, then call time.

Do the "Light of the World" station as a group so people can further explore the power of Jesus' forgiveness and commit to giving that forgiveness to others.

HERE'S WHAT TO DO

- Make sure everyone has a small candle (or have the candles in a basket or other container).

  SAY "Jesus shouted, 'Father, I entrust my spirit into your hands!' And with those words he breathed his last." Jesus, the Son of God, died for our sins. But that wasn't the end of the story! Three days later, Jesus rose from the dead. He came back to life—so we can have life with him forever.

- Light the pillar candle with the lighter or match.

- Read:

  SAY In John 8:12, Jesus says "I am the light of the world. If you follow me, you won't have to walk in darkness, because you will have the light that leads to life."

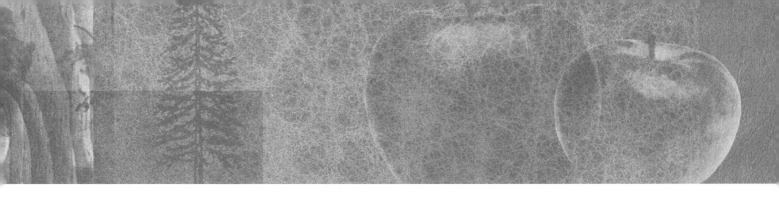

- Walk to the candleholder, and place the lit pillar candle there. (Be careful, because moving quickly will cause the flame to go out.)

- Take a small candle, light it from the pillar candle, and set the small candle on the tablecloth beside the pillar candle.

- Read aloud:

  SAY In Matthew 5:14-16, Jesus says, "You are the light of the world—like a city on a hilltop that cannot be hidden. No one lights a lamp and then puts it under a basket. Instead, a lamp is placed on a stand, where it gives light to everyone in the house. In the same way, let your good deeds shine out for all to see, so that everyone will praise your heavenly Father."

  Please light your candle from one of the other small candles as a sign of the life and light you have in Jesus. Place your candle near the pillar candle as a commitment to forgive others and share Jesus' forgiveness. Then step back or sit down and reflect or pray quietly.

- If possible, turn the lights completely out after explaining this part of the Station 7. Spend the next one or two minutes in darkness, watching as all the candles are lit.

- After everyone has finished lighting the candles, have one or two minutes of quiet reflection as the music continues to play in the background.

- After a few moments of silent prayer and reflection, close with a prayer.

  PRAY Jesus, thank you for bringing light into our darkness so that we might experience your transforming forgiveness and love. Help us forgive others and spread your light into the world. Amen.

- Have everyone blow out the candles.

Lighting a candle to show that in Jesus we have light and life

Daily Challenge ™

The Daily Challenges will give people an opportunity to practice what they explored during the week's Get-Together.

HERE'S WHAT TO DO

- Have everyone go to page 134 of the *Friendship First* book. Have a volunteer read the "Experience Forgiveness" Daily Challenges aloud.

- Have everyone choose one of the challenges to do in the coming week and mark it in the book. Ask people to take turns around the room telling which challenge they plan to do.

- Have people take home the small candles, which symbolize Jesus' forgiveness and love. They should use this candle as a tangible reminder to follow through on the Daily Challenge.

- Tell everyone to be ready to report how the Daily Challenge went next time the group meets.

- Encourage everyone to continue reading Chapter 5 of the *Friendship First* book throughout the week.

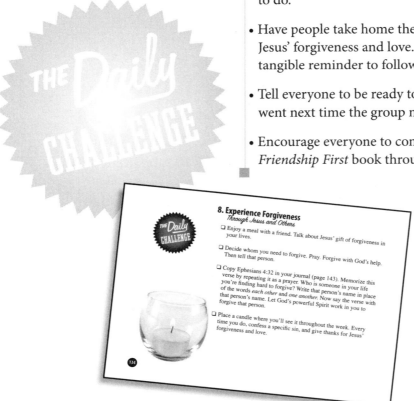

8. Experience Forgiveness
Through Jesus and Others

❏ Enjoy a meal with a friend. Talk about Jesus' gift of forgiveness in your lives.

❏ Decide whom you need to forgive. Pray. Forgive with God's help. Then tell that person.

❏ Copy Ephesians 4:32 in your journal (page 143). Memorize this verse by repeating it as a prayer. Who is someone in your life you're finding hard to forgive? Write that person's name in place of the words *each other* and *one another*. Now say the verse with that person's name. Let God's powerful Spirit work in you to forgive that person.

❏ Place a candle where you'll see it throughout the week. Every time you do, confess a specific sin, and give thanks for Jesus' forgiveness and love.

134

The Painful Thorns

Before his death, Jesus received a crown of thorns.

Hold the object and run your thumb over its point. As you feel the sharpness, thank Jesus for enduring the pain on the cross and for taking on the thorns in your life. Pray that God will take away the pain that you suffer from not forgiving others.

The Spike of Sin

The Roman soldiers hammered spikes into Jesus' hands and feet.

Strike nails with a hammer and ask for forgiveness for a specific sin in your life.

The Bitter Vinegar

While hanging on the cross, Jesus was offered a taste of vinegar for his thirst.

Dip a cotton swab in the vinegar and reflect on bitter times in your life. Pray that God will help you to forgive, give you a soft and sweet heart toward others, and remove your bitterness.

Distracting Dice

The soldiers gambled for Jesus' robe, throwing dice for his clothing, ignoring the Son of God who hung nearby.

Roll a single die. Look at the number that comes up and name that many of the distractions that keep you from experiencing Jesus' forgiveness. Pray that God will help you focus on Jesus instead.

Remember Me

One of the thieves hanging beside Jesus begged him to "Remember me" in heaven. The red ink symbolizes Jesus' blood shed for you.

Write your name under the words "Remember me," and thank Jesus for forgiving you and loving you eternally.

The New Agreement With God

The Temple once had a thick curtain that divided the Holy Place, where the people could go, from the Most Holy Place, where God was. When Jesus died, the curtain ripped from top to bottom. There was no more separation between God and us. When the army officer who was standing in front of the cross saw what had happened when Jesus died, he said, "This man truly was the Son of God!"

Tear a piece of the cloth, and thank God for ripping through that barrier in your life so that you may be friends with Jesus.

GET-TOGETHER 9

Value the little things with Jesus and others.

PSALM 145:13B-21

The "everydayness" of being a good friend can be tough. We've all got responsibilities, work, and chores that take our time and attention, and it's all too easy to let our friendships slide. Each day we busily take care of the urgent, and before we know it, weeks or months can go by without even an e-mail to our friends. Who has time to nurture friendships each day? Our Best Friend does! He knows that the little things matter. Jesus cares so much about us that he numbered our days before we were born. Jesus has a plan for us, and he is actively involved in the details of our everyday life. That's right! The great big God, who created the multitude of galaxies that make up the universe, cares about each detail of your life. Wow! We can strive to be as attentive and caring with our earthly friends. The people in our lives are worth our time, our attention, and our love every day.

Get-Together at a Glance

	WHAT PEOPLE WILL DO	MINUTES	SUPPLIES
CAFÉ TIME	Eat a snack or meal that connects with today's point. OPTIONS *(Choose One)*: ☐ *Quick and Easy:* Mini-Snacks ☐ *Easy Plus:* Assorted Cheese Cubes ☐ *High Impact:* Mini-Meatballs and Mini-Sausages	 10 to 15 30 60	See pp. 183-184 for details
EXPERIENCING FRIENDSHIP	*Sweet or Sour* Eat sweet or sour candy and share about sweet or sour relationships.	10 to 12	• Sweet candies such as M&M's candies • Sour candy such as sour Skittles • bowl • napkin
	Quick-Change Artist Play a game where they must notice little changes about each other.	10 to 12	
	Graciousness Talk about how to treat others with graciousness in the little things of life.	10 to 12	• *Friendship First* books • paper • pens • *Friendship First* DVD • DVD player
PRAYER	Consider God's care as they hold various objects, and pray in response to Psalm 145.	5 to 10	• Bible • various items (see p. 122) • tray • *Friendship First* CD • CD player
DAILY CHALLENGE	Talk about the Daily Challenges they'll carry out during the week.	up to 5	• *Friendship First* books • pens • miniature candy bars

GET-TOGETHER
9

Value the little things with Jesus and others.

What friendship doesn't include eating together? Food is a very important part of the Friendship First experience. As we eat together, we grow closer together—we relax, we smile, we share. It's the perfect beginning to each friendship Get-Together. Remember that during these Get-Togethers, your focus is on people. Take the time to enjoy the fellowship of the table together.

We've provided three delicious options for each week's Get-Together. Choose the one that best fits your time, your setting, and your budget. See pages 183-184 for details on today's menu options.

Music IDEAS

Set a great atmosphere by playing background music that matches the mood of this Get-Together! Here are some genre suggestions:
- light classical
- upbeat praise
- alternative
- acoustic rock

You can also play the Friendship First theme song, "Here for You" (track 11 on the *Friendship First* CD).

Café Time

PURPOSE

Today's Get-Together is about valuing the little things in our friendships with Jesus and others. All of today's food options include tidbits of food.

☐ *QUICK AND EASY*
Mini-Snacks

or

☐ *EASY PLUS*
Assorted Cheese Cubes

or

☐ *HIGH IMPACT*
Mini-Meatballs & Sausages

HERE'S WHAT TO DO

- Make sure that each person feels welcome and at home at today's Get-Together. You may personally welcome each person, or if you'll be busy getting the last-minute details organized, find a warm, friendly person to be the greeter.

- If you're using the **Quick and Easy** or **Easy Plus** option, invite people to get a snack before they sit down in their groups of six.

- If you're using the **High Impact** option, wait until everyone's arrived.

- Ask the blessing.

- Have everyone fill a plate, sit down, and begin eating.

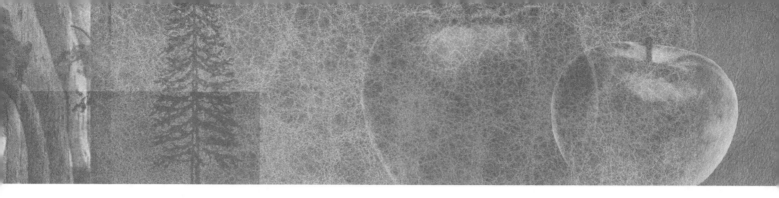

- While everyone's eating, allow for small talk and casual chatting.

- At some point in the conversation, discuss Chapter 5 in the *Friendship First* book. Ask people what struck them most in what they read.

- After a few minutes of discussion (or when there's a natural break in the conversation), discuss the significance of the food.

 ASK **What could the food we're eating today symbolize about friendship? Let's think of as many possibilities as we can.**

SAY **These are all great insights into friendship. Everything we ate today was small—just little tidbits of food. Today we'll be talking about how the little things in our friendships really matter. We'll also discover that God is interested in all the little details of our lives.**

Now let's check in on the Daily Challenges. How did you follow through with your Daily Challenge commitment? What happened as a result?

- Thank everyone for sharing a Daily Challenge story.

 INSIDE SCOOP One exciting development this week was that people started talking about how important their growing relationships with one another were. The participants started making plans to meet after the Friendship First Get-Togethers were over.

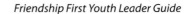

EXPERIENCING Friendship

Sweet or Sour

This story-sharing activity will help people get to know one another better. It will also help to introduce the topic by having people talk about their own experiences, which will help them connect emotionally to today's discussion. This emotional connection will help to reinforce the point of today's Get-Together.

HERE'S WHAT TO DO

- Form pairs.

- Pass around a bowl of candy (M&M's and Sour Skittles), which you've covered with a napkin or cloth, and have people close their eyes, take one candy, and put it in their mouths.

- If the chosen candy is sweet, the person should tell his or her partner about a sweet time with a friend or with God. If the candy is sour, the person should tell about a sour time with a friend or with God.

- After both partners have had a chance to share at least one story, have pairs discuss these questions:

ASK **Was the story you told your partner about big, significant things or small, everyday things?**

Why are the little things such a big deal in our relationships?

Sour or sweet? We've all experienced both in our relationships!

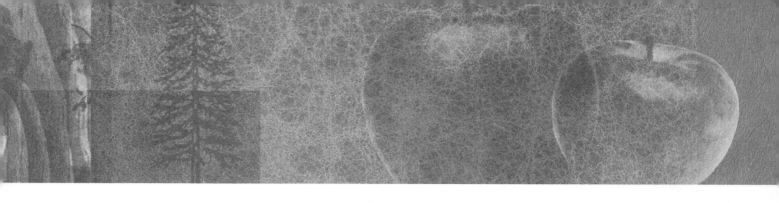

2 *Quick-Change Artist*

This is a fun game that will help everyone start to pay attention to the details and discuss why the little things matter.

HERE'S WHAT TO DO

- Form pairs.

- Have pairs sit back to back. Have one partner change something about his or her appearance—for example, take off one earring or zip up a jacket.

- Have the partners turn around to face each other. Have the other partner guess what the first partner changed about his or her appearance.

- Have the partners trade roles and play again.

- Have pairs discuss these questions:

  ASK Did you find it easy or difficult to notice a small change in your partner's appearance? Explain.

  In our friendships, what kinds of details should we be paying attention to?

  What small details are important in our relationship with God?

  SAY Before we go on to our next activity, tell your partner one little thing you appreciate about him or her.

- Give pairs time to share with each other.

Noticing little changes isn't all that easy.

3

Graciousness

This activity will give everyone an opportunity to talk about how to treat others with honor, graciousness, and love.

HERE'S WHAT TO DO

 SAY **There are lots of little ways we can let people know that they're important to us—ways we can treat others with honor, graciousness, and love. Sometimes we call these little things courtesy or good manners.**

In a moment, you'll have a chance to create your own list of good manners for relationships. To help you start thinking about what to write, I've got some quotations for you to read and talk about.

• Have everyone turn to the courtesy quotations on page 66 of the *Friendship First* book. Have one person read each quotation aloud.

• After the quotations have been read aloud, provide pens and have people underline a phrase or a word in one of the quotations that caught their attention and then share what they underlined with a partner.

• Discuss these questions:

 ASK **What insights can you glean from these quotations about how to treat others?**

Treating others well seems like an elementary part of friendship. Why is it necessary and good to discuss manners and how to treat others?

• Provide paper. Have the group work together to come up with a list of good manners for relationships.

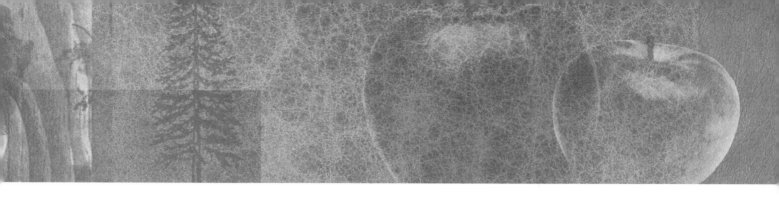

- When you have a list, discuss these questions:

  ASK **What effect would using these manners in our friendships have on our friends and on us?**

  Look over the list of manners. How does each one, or the principle behind it, relate to your relationship with God?

- Show segment 5, "The Little Things," on the *Friendship First* DVD.

- After the DVD segment, discuss these questions:

  ASK **How does knowing that God cares about and is involved in all the small details of your life make you feel?**

  How have you noticed God's gracious care of the details of your life?

Friendship First™ Gathering Cards and Nature Cards are a great way to show love and concern for the people in your group. Order at www.friendshipfirst.com.

Prayer

This prayer activity will help everyone consider how God has paid attention to the little things in his or her own life.

HERE'S WHAT TO DO

- Before the Get-Together, gather at least four or five of the following items: a leaf, sandpaper, a square of soft fabric such as velvet, a feather, a glass of water, a slice of bread, cotton batting, a bandage, a rock, a travel pillow, or facial tissue. Put all the items on a tray.

SAY **Listen to these words from Scripture:**

"The Lord is merciful and compassionate, slow to get angry and filled with unfailing love. The Lord is good to everyone. He showers compassion on all his creation. All of your works will thank you, Lord, and your faithful followers will praise you" (Psalm 145:8-10).

SAY **God is a gracious gentleman—he pays attention to the small things and the large things in our lives. He never forgets or neglects us.**

- Have everyone think about his or her relationship with God.

- Put the tray in the middle of the group. Ask everyone to pass the items around the group slowly and prayerfully while silently and prayerfully considering how each item symbolizes God's attention to the small things in his or her life. For example, someone might hold the bandage and recognize God's help when he or she had a cold. Or maybe someone will hold the cotton batting and think about God's gentle comfort after a bad dream.

- When all the items have been passed around the group and returned to the tray, have people turn to a partner and share how God has been graciously involved in the details of their lives.

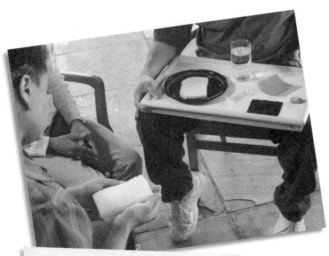

Seeing God in these everyday items helps participants see God every day!

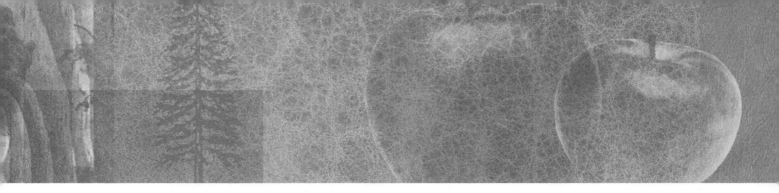

- Get everyone's attention.

SAY **I'm going to read a passage from Scripture. I'll pause periodically and give you time to pray about what I've just read.**

- Read Psalm 145:13b-21, pausing when indicated for everyone to pray.

> **"The Lord always keeps his promises** (pause);
>
> **he is gracious in all he does.** (Pause.)
>
> **The Lord helps the fallen and lifts those bent beneath their loads.** (Pause.)
>
> **The eyes of all look to you in hope** (pause);
>
> **You give them their food as they need it. When you open your hand, you satisfy the hunger and thirst of every living thing.** (Pause.)
>
> **The Lord is righteous in everything he does; he is filled with kindness.** (Pause.)
>
> **The Lord is close to all who call on him, yes, to all who call on him in truth.** (Pause.)
>
> **He grants the desires of those who fear him** (pause);
>
> **he hears their cries for help and rescues them.** (Pause.)
>
> **The Lord protects all those who love him, but he destroys the wicked.** (Pause.)
>
> **I will praise the Lord, and may everyone on earth bless his holy name forever and ever."** (Pause.)

- End your time together by playing track 8, "His Eye Is on the Sparrow" on the *Friendship First* CD. Invite everyone to continue to pray while listening to the song.

GET-TOGETHER 9

Value the little things with Jesus and others.

Daily Challenge™

This activity will help people practice what they've learned about friendship.

HERE'S WHAT TO DO

- Have people turn to page 135 in their *Friendship First* books. Have a volunteer read the "Value the Little Things" Daily Challenges aloud.

- Have everyone choose one of the challenges to do in the coming week and mark it in the book. Have people take turns around the room telling which challenge they plan to do.

- Give everyone a miniature candy bar as a reminder to value the little things in his or her relationships with Jesus and others while doing the Daily Challenge.

- Tell everyone to be ready to report how the Daily Challenge went next time you meet.

- Encourage everyone to continue to read Chapter 5 of the book during the week.

Between Friends

This would be a good week to start planning the fun outing your group will enjoy together during Get-Together 11. See page 138 for details. Mention it to the group this week, and plan to make more definite plans next week.

9. Value the Little Things
With Jesus and Others

☐ Pay attention to the little details of good relationships by making a special effort to exhibit good manners this week at home, school, work—wherever you are. Say, "Please," "Thank you," and "Excuse me." See what happens!

☐ Be gracious to others by showing extra care. Remember a birthday by taking out a friend, send a letter on real stationery, take a bouquet of flowers to a friend, let someone else go in line first.

☐ Place your comb or hairbrush in an unusual place. Put it on your Bible, opened to Matthew 10:29-31. Let this remind you all week that God cares about the little things—even the hairs on your head! (Also use it as an opportunity to talk about your friendship with God with your curious friends or members of your family who wonder what you're up to!)

☐ God cares about the details! Check out 1 Peter 5:7. Memorize that verse by praying it throughout one entire day. Make God a part of your entire day—through the big and small stuff. Imagine God is right there beside you, every moment. At the end of the day, use your journal (page 143) to record your impressions.

135

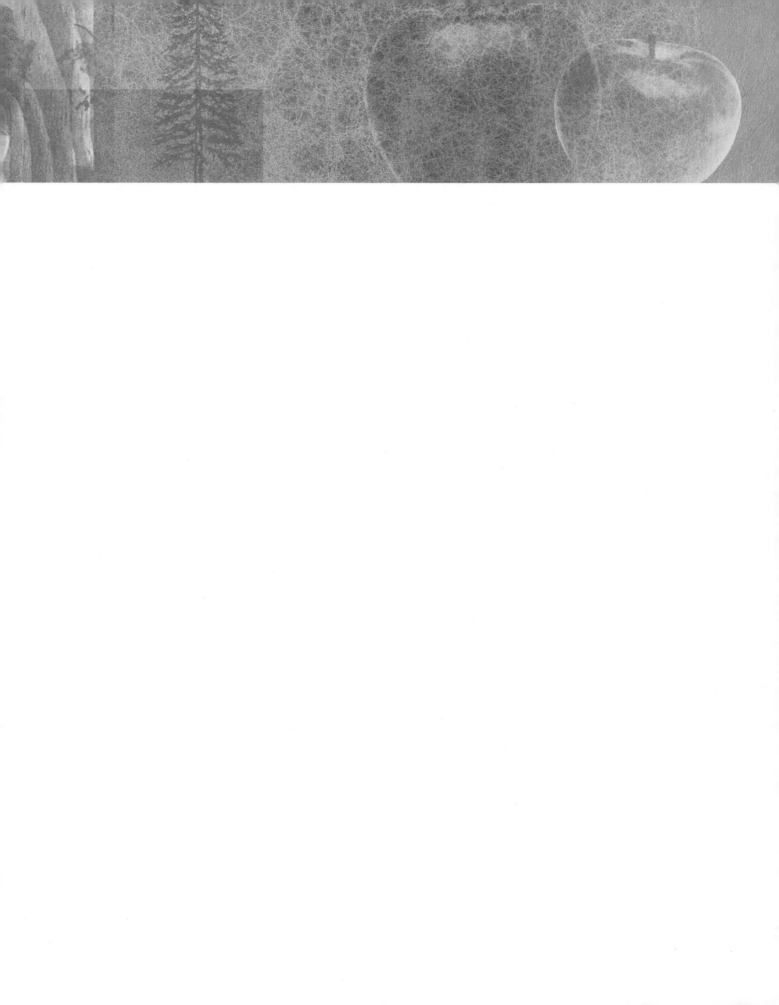

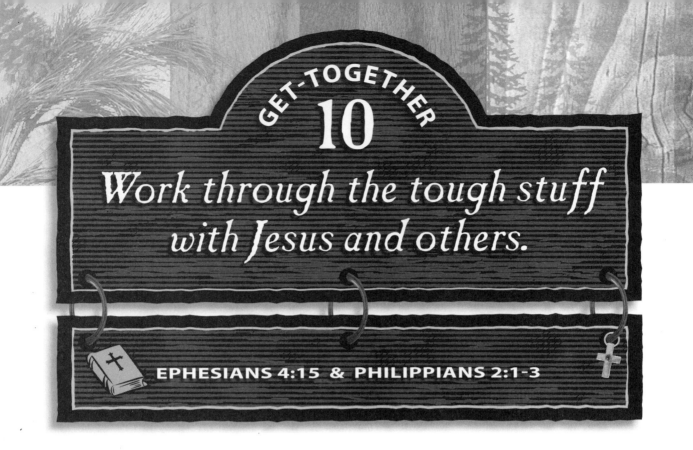

GET-TOGETHER
10
Work through the tough stuff with Jesus and others.

EPHESIANS 4:15 & PHILIPPIANS 2:1-3

Let's face it—friendships are messy. Even in healthy friendships, people disappoint, disagree, and hurt each other's feelings. But that's what makes the journey of friendship such a vivid, rewarding adventure. And it's such a wonderful opportunity to grow closer to someone else in real intimacy, since friendships are actually strengthened through all the messiness. Today your group members will discover together how, instead of running away from tough times, you can go through tough times with deeper trust and joy from God.

Get-Together at a Glance

	WHAT PEOPLE WILL DO	MINUTES	SUPPLIES
**CAFÉ TIME**	Eat a snack or meal that connects with today's point. OPTIONS *(Choose One)*: ☐ *Quick and Easy:* Powdered Sugar Doughnuts ☐ *Easy Plus:* S'mores ☐ *High Impact:* Cajun Boil	10 to 15 30 60	See pp. 185-186 for details
EXPERIENCING FRIENDSHIP	▼ *Just Say It* Practice saying the hard thing to a friend, then discuss healthy ways to handle messiness in friendship.	10 to 12	• *Friendship First* book for each person
	▼ *Stretching* Do an object lesson together, and explore ways Jesus "stretches" us in friendship.	10 to 12	• 1 thick, wide rubber band
	▼ *Together* Move to represent what happens in friendships, and be affirmed for being like Jesus to others.	10 to 12	• Bible
**PRAYER**	Pray about messy friendships and tough situations.	5 to 10	• 1 small rubber band for each person
DAILY CHALLENGE	Talk about the Daily Challenges they'll carry out during the week.	up to 5	• *Friendship First* books

*Work through
the tough stuff
with Jesus and others.*

What friendship doesn't
include eating together?
*Food is a very important part of
the Friendship First experience. As
we eat together, we grow closer
together—we relax, we smile,
we share. It's the perfect beginning
to each friendship Get-Together.
Remember that during these
Get-Togethers, your focus is on
people. Take the time to enjoy the
fellowship of the table together.*

*We've provided three delicious
options for each week's Get-
Together. Choose the one that best
fits your time, your setting, and
your budget. See pages 185-186 for
details on today's menu options.*

Café Time

PURPOSE
*Food that is messy will lead into a discussion on messiness
and tough times in friendships.*

☐ *QUICK AND EASY*
Powdered Sugar Doughnuts

or

☐ *EASY PLUS*
S'mores

or

☐ *HIGH IMPACT*
Cajun Boil

Music
IDEAS

Set a great atmosphere by playing
background music that matches the
mood of this Get-Together! Here are
some genre suggestions:

- blues
- R&B
- gospel
- reggae

You can also play the Friendship First
theme song, "Here for You" (track 11
on the *Friendship First* CD).

HERE'S WHAT TO DO

- Make sure that each person feels welcome and at home at today's
  Get-Together. You may personally welcome each person, or if
  you'll be busy getting the last-minute details organized, find a
  warm, friendly person to be the greeter.

- If you're using the **Quick and Easy** or **Easy Plus** option, invite
  people to get a snack before they sit down in their groups of six.

- If you're using the **High Impact** option, wait until
  everyone's arrived.

- Ask the blessing.

- Have everyone fill a plate, sit down, and begin eating.

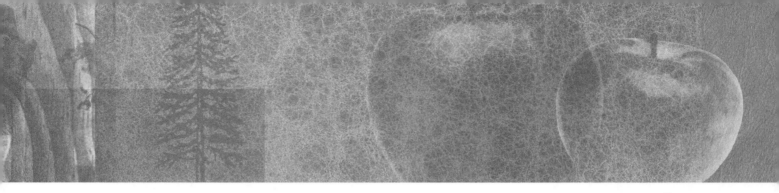

- While everyone's eating, allow for small talk and casual chatting.

- At some point in the conversation, continue discussing Chapter 5 in *Friendship First*. Ask people what struck them most in what they read.

- After a few minutes of discussion (or when there's a natural break in the conversation), discuss the significance of the food.

ASK **What could the food we're eating today symbolize about friendship? Let's think of as many possibilities as we can.**

SAY **Thanks for all your ideas! Our food today is messy and is sort of a challenge to eat. Besides making us throw away everything we learned last time about manners…** (smile).

Today we're going to discuss the ways friendships are messy. We'll talk about how we are disappointed and how we disappoint others, and we'll explore how Jesus helps us be authentic and loving, even when it means saying the hard thing.

First let's check in on the Daily Challenges. How did you follow through with your Daily Challenge commitment? What happened as a result?

- Thank everyone for sharing a Daily Challenge story.

Between Friends

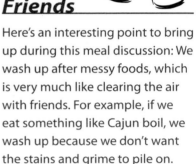

Here's an interesting point to bring up during this meal discussion: We wash up after messy foods, which is very much like clearing the air with friends. For example, if we eat something like Cajun boil, we wash up because we don't want the stains and grime to pile on. Likewise, we clean up with friends so that other kinds of stains and grime don't pile on.

GET-TOGETHER

10

*Work through
the tough stuff
with Jesus and others.*

EXPERIENCING Friendship

Just Say It

In this activity, people will talk about reasons friendships are messy and practice saying "the hard thing" to a friend.

HERE'S WHAT TO DO

- Have everyone open to page 68 in the *Friendship First* book and read together the "Confront Disagreements" section.

- Discuss these questions:

   ASK **What idea stands out to you most from this reading? Why?**

  In addition to anger, what are other things that make a friendship messy?

- After brainstorming,

  SAY **Because we're human, our friendships are messy. There are lots of reasons. Sometimes we hurt or are hurt; sometimes we push away or are pushed away; sometimes we don't forgive or aren't forgiven.**

- Discuss these questions:

  ASK **What do you think are healthy or unhealthy ways to handle these disappointments in a friendship?**

  How is your relationship with Jesus messy sometimes?

- Have people form pairs.

- Have partners turn to page 72 of the *Friendship First* books and look at the box with the heading "As a friend, what would you do?" This box includes four difficult, real-life scenarios:

- Your friend broke a confidence and shared your secret. You found out. What would you say to your friend?

  1. *You know your relationship isn't working, and you've decided to call it quits. How will you explain that you want to break up?*

Saying the hard thing is difficult and takes practice!

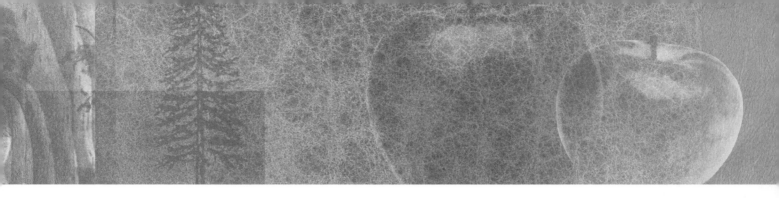

2. *You've just learned your friend has chosen a lifestyle you disagree with. How will you tell your friend your feelings?*

3. *You just did something you know will hurt your friend deeply. How will you ask for forgiveness?*

- Tell pairs that each person will choose one scenario.

- Each partner will take one minute to practice what he or she would say to someone in this situation.

- Have the first partner practice saying the hard thing, then call time after one minute.

- Have partners switch so that the other partner talks, and call time after another minute.

- Discuss the experience:

ASK **What were you thinking and feeling?**

How was this like or unlike saying the hard thing to a friend?

How is a messy human friendship like a messy relationship with God?

- Read aloud Ephesians 4:15:

"**We will hold to the truth in love, becoming more and more in every way like Christ, who is the head of his body, the church.**"

ASK **How can we hold to truth and love in messy friendships?**

How might saying the hard thing cause you to grow closer to others and Jesus?

Extend this discussion by exploring what a friend might do when saying the hard thing just isn't enough. Gather ideas, and talk about practical ways someone might encourage a friend or tell truth to a friend in a tough situation.

INSIDE SCOOP Our discussions included the struggle that occurs when friends go in a direction you don't want to go (such as drugs or drinking). Talk with teenagers about the messiness that happens when people associate you with these friends.

Between Friends

This is a great time to order a 1 Thing lapel pin for each group member. You'll need these pins during Get-Together 13.

Order by calling 1-800-747-6060 ext. 1370. Or order online at www.friendshipfirst.com.

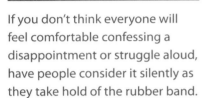

Between Friends

If you don't think everyone will feel comfortable confessing a disappointment or struggle aloud, have people consider it silently as they take hold of the rubber band.

Don't worry if the rubber band breaks as everyone pulls on it; this will provide a great opportunity to talk about how Jesus uses friendships to ease our pain when we reach our own "breaking point." (After all, a snapped rubber band hurts a lot less with several people holding it rather than just one!)

Stretching

Do this rubber-band activity together to practice authenticity and explore how God uses friendships to "stretch" us toward Jesus.

HERE'S WHAT TO DO

- Have everyone form a circle.

- Set the rubber band in the middle of the circle. Then grab hold of one side of it (it might be best to use two fingers), and describe a struggle or disappointment. The description doesn't have to be intimate—it should be vague and shouldn't use names—but the struggle should be something that's difficult to talk about and requires authenticity. For instance, you might say, "I've been let down," or "I don't feel spiritually good enough."

- Have each person, one by one, grab part of the rubber band and confess a disappointment to the group.

- Have everyone pull outward gently so that the rubber band stretches.

- While everyone holds the rubber band, discuss these questions:

   ASK **How is this like or unlike the ways we are "stretched" in friendship?**

  How does Jesus challenge us to be more authentic with him and others?

- Have everyone let go of the rubber band and turn to the same partner as before to discuss these questions. (Pause between questions to give partners time to talk.)

   ASK **Through which messy friendship or experience is Jesus stretching you?**

  How will you respond?

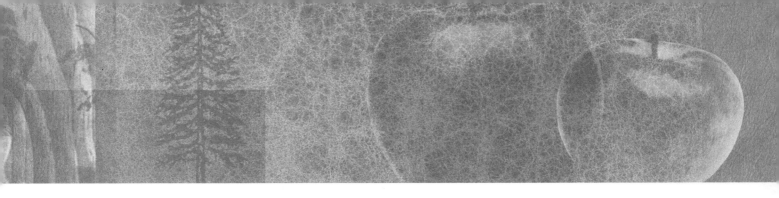

Together

Lead group members through this powerful experience, which illustrates real relationships and also affirms the people in your group for persevering in friendship and representing Jesus to others.

HERE'S WHAT TO DO

- Have group members again form a circle and stand up.

- Have people hold hands.

  SAY **Friendship is fun, hopeful, and encouraging. But it's not always that way. Sometimes it's also disappointing, painful, and messy.**

- Pause for a moment. Then continue, thoughtfully and prayerfully.

  SAY **Sometimes we separate ourselves from each other and can't enjoy the love God intends for us.** (Pause briefly.)

  If you have ever been disappointed in a friendship, or if you have disappointed someone, please drop your arms to your sides. (Pause.)

  Sometimes we say things that are harmful to others. (Pause briefly.)

  I'd like anyone who's ever said something harmful to a friend to take a step backward. (Pause.)

  Often we push others away.

  If anyone has ever pushed someone away or been pushed away, please take a step backward. (Pause.)

  Sometimes we say something that's not true or don't say what needs to be said. We aren't authentic or loving in telling somebody the truth. (Pause briefly.)

  If this has ever happened to you, I'd like you to turn and face away from the center of the circle. (Pause.)

What a powerful group experience!

Sometimes we pretend not to see the needs of other people. (Pause briefly.)

If there have been times you've ignored the needs of others and haven't reached out to them, please close your eyes and keep them closed. (Pause.)

We're meant to have close friendships, yet at times our struggles and disappointments keep us apart. (Pause briefly.)

If you've ever helped someone with a need or reached out to someone, I'd like you to turn around. (Pause.)

If you've ever taken the time to listen to a friend who was struggling, please take one step in. (Pause.)

If you've ever built someone up with encouraging words, open your eyes. (Pause.)

If you've ever shared a way that you failed someone, even though it was hard to say, take another step in. (Pause.)

God asks us to forgive one another. (Pause briefly.)

If you've ever forgiven someone, take the hands of the people next to you.

- After a few moments of reflective silence, read aloud Philippians 2:1-3:

"Is there any encouragement from belonging to Christ? Any comfort from his love? Any fellowship together in the Spirit? Are your hearts tender and compassionate? Then make me truly happy by agreeing wholeheartedly with each other, loving one another, and working together with one heart and purpose.

Don't be selfish; don't try to impress others. Be humble, thinking of others as better than yourself."

- After a few more moments of silence, continue on to the prayer time.

Prayer

In this simple prayer activity, people will acknowledge the gift of friendship in their lives and surrender specific "messiness" to God, asking that they would show Jesus' love through the tough stuff.

HERE'S WHAT TO DO

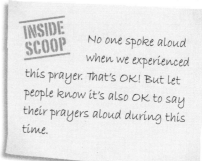

INSIDE SCOOP No one spoke aloud when we experienced this prayer. That's OK! But let people know it's also OK to say their prayers aloud during this time.

- Give each person a small rubber band.

SAY Friendships are messy, complicated, and sometimes painful. But they are precious gifts from God, and he uses them to stretch us and to bring us closer to Jesus. Right now, I'd like you to take a few moments to think about a friendship in which loving the friend means you have to say a really hard thing. It may be Jesus or someone else in your life. Perhaps you need to confess something, or you may need to tell that person the truth in love. As you hold this rubber band, symbolizing how Jesus is working in your life, explore the friendship and the situation in prayer right now. Bring them to God, and ask that he would stretch you and guide you to be authentic and loving.

- Have everyone spend a few moments in prayer.

- Then close with a prayer:

PRAY Jesus, thank you for stretching us and challenging us so that we might become more like you. We acknowledge that we contribute to our messy friendships by hurting and disappointing others and by sometimes not saying what should be said. Please help us not to run away but to go through friendships no matter what. Show us how to share truth in love, and make us truly authentic friends, with you and with others. Amen.

**Work through
the tough stuff
with Jesus and others.**

Daily Challenge ™

The Daily Challenge will give people an opportunity to practice what they explored during the week's Get-Together.

Between Friends

Be sure to spend some time today making plans for next week's fun outing. See page 138 for details.

HERE'S WHAT TO DO

- Have everyone go to page 136 of *Friendship First*. Have a volunteer read the Daily Challenges aloud.

- Have everyone choose one of the challenges to do in the coming week and mark it in the book. Ask people to take turns around the room telling which challenge they plan to do.

- Have people take home the rubber bands, which symbolize the ways Jesus helps them through tough situations, and use them as a tangible reminder to follow through on the Daily Challenge.

- Tell everyone to be ready to report how the Daily Challenge went next time the group meets.

- Encourage everyone to begin reading Chapter 6 of *Friendship First* during the week.

Be flexible, like a rubber band.

10. Work Through the Tough Stuff
With Jesus and Others

☐ Invite a friend over to help you clean your garage, bedroom, closet, attic—anything that's a mess. While you're working together, talk about how cleaning up a messy place is like or unlike cleaning up messy relationships.

☐ Write a letter to someone with whom you need to make amends. Pray about saying the right things; then call or meet that person and share what you wrote. Clean up the mess in the friendship.

☐ Read Matthew 18:15-17. Reflect on the times you've failed to go directly to someone who has wronged you. Confess those times to God. Plan to put Matthew 18:15-17 into action the next time a messy situation occurs. Depend upon God to bless your efforts.

☐ Find a full wastebasket. Place it in front of you and pray. Let it spark a prayer that speaks of disappointments and hurts in your relationships. Ask God to clean up the mess and heal the hurts.

136

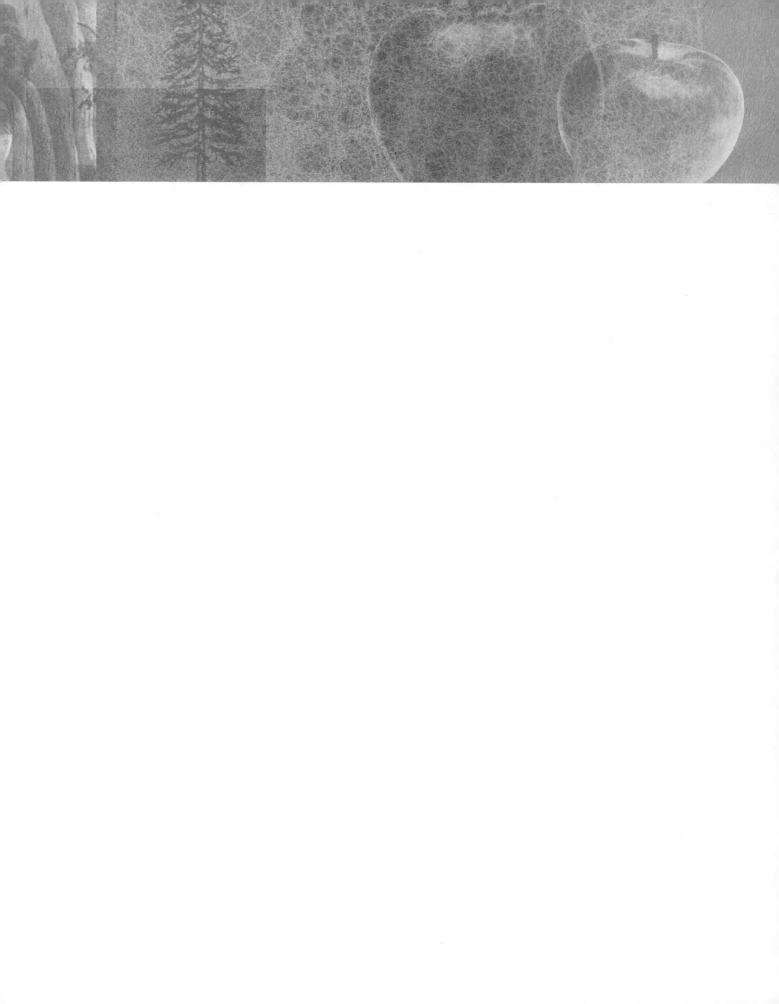

GET-TOGETHER

11

Enjoy time with Jesus and others.

ECCLESIASTES 4:9

Companionship is an important part of any friendship! Friends are people we like to spend time with, laughing and having fun together. Today's Get-Together is an opportunity to enjoy the company of your Friendship First group. Plan to enjoy a time of fun, food, and fellowship together.

Get-Together at a Glance

	WHAT PEOPLE WILL DO	MINUTES	SUPPLIES

CAFÉ TIME

Potluck

If the group would like to enjoy a meal together, invite everyone to bring a favorite dish to share.

EXPERIENCING FRIENDSHIP

Fun Time

Enjoy a time of fellowship. Choose a fun activity to do together.

FRIENDSHIP DEVOTIONS

OPTION 1: *Circle of Friends*

Play a game where one person tries to break into a circle of people whose elbows are locked. — up to 5

OPTION 2: *Connected One to Another*

Toss around a ball in a game that illustrates how interconnected we are. — up to 5

- Soft ball
- rubber bands

OPTION 3: *Come On In*

Listen to a song about being a part of God's family. — up to 5

- *Friendship First* CD
- CD player

Café Time

*If you
meet for a meal
today, have a
potluck. Encourage
everyone to bring
a favorite dish
to share.*

EXPERIENCING Friendship

Your primary goal for today's Get-Together is to have fun! But you'll also want to reinforce the friendship principles you've been exploring during the past 10 weeks.

HERE ARE SOME IDEAS TO HELP YOU DO THAT:

- Have everyone find a partner to stick with during the Get-Together. Have partners work on getting to know each other better.

- Have everyone be on the lookout for friendship in action during your Get-Together. At the end of the event, invite everyone to share how he or she saw friendship being expressed throughout your Get-Together.

- Invite people to draw names and then, at some time during the fun, express love and appreciation for the person whose name they've drawn.

- If your fun event involves teams, minimize any feeling of competition by having each team do something to serve and love the other team at some point during the event.

- Encourage further fun and friendship! Before the night's over, encourage the group to make plans for another fun outing.

At the end of your fun time together, encourage everyone to look up the "Enjoy Time With Jesus and Others" Daily Challenges on page 137 of *Friendship First* when they get home. Suggest that everyone choose at least one challenge to do this week.

Fun Time

Today's Get-Together is all about having fun together and enjoying one another's companionship.

HERE ARE SOME ACTIVITY IDEAS:

- **go bowling**

- **play miniature golf**

- **go to a video arcade**

- **hike or snowshoe on a local trail**

- **go water-skiing or ice-skating**

- **go on a scavenger hunt**

- **play board games or cards at someone's home** ▼

- **play soccer or baseball at the park**

- **contact your church to find a service project, such as painting someone's home or raking someone's yard**

Friendship DEVOTIONS

You may want to use one or more of these optional devotion ideas before or after your fun event. Be aware that Option 2 and Option 3 require some easy-to-find supplies.

OPTION 1: *Circle of Friends*

This activity will help everyone understand the importance of being included in the companionship of friends.

HERE'S WHAT TO DO

Participants discover what it means to include others.

- Have all but one person stand in a circle and hook elbows to lock their arms together.

- Have the person standing on the outside of the circle try to get inside it, while everyone standing in the circle tries to keep him or her out.

- Whether or not the person is successful, discuss these questions:

   ASK **What were you thinking and feeling during this activity?**

  What did this activity illustrate about companionship and friendship?

  How can we relate these insights to our relationship with Jesus?

OPTION 2: *Connected One to Another*

This game will help everyone see how interconnected we are.

HERE'S WHAT TO DO

- Have everyone stand in a circle.

- Give each person a rubber band. Have people use the rubber bands to join their wrists to a neighbor's wrist so that everyone is connected wrist to wrist around the circle.

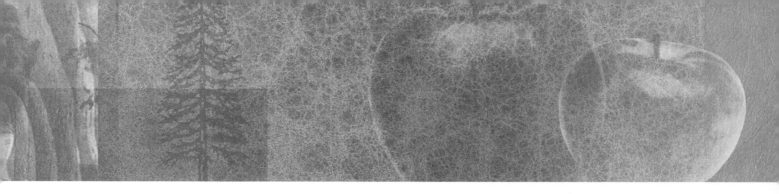

- Toss a soft ball to someone in the circle. Have people toss the ball back and forth across the circle for a minute or two.

- Stop the game. Have everyone stay connected while you discuss these questions:

ASK **What were you thinking and feeling while we played this game?**

What does this game teach about friendship?

How can you relate these truths about friendship to our relationship with Jesus?

Participants learn the importance of being connected to others.

OPTION 3: *Come On In*

This song will help everyone see the importance of being a part of "the circle."

HERE'S WHAT TO DO

- Have a volunteer read John 15:15 aloud.

- Cue the *Friendship First* CD to track 9, "Come On In."

SAY **Let's listen to this song about a circle of friends prayerfully. Talk to God about your friendship with him and others during this song.**

- Have people stand in a circle, hold hands, and stay connected while they listen to the song prayerfully.

- Play the song.

- Close your devotion time in prayer, asking God to help you deepen your friendships with others and with Jesus.

Friendship First™ Gathering Cards and Nature Cards are a great way to show love and concern for the people in your group. Order at www.friendshipfirst.com.

GET-TOGETHER

12

Stick with Jesus and others.

2 CORINTHIANS 5:14-15

The most important ingredient in a treasured, lifelong friendship is commitment. Committing to someone else in a friendship means investing fully, loving unconditionally, being faithful and dedicated through all seasons or circumstances, and sticking with that person no matter what happens. This is the kind of fully committed friend Jesus is to us. Through the experiences in this Get-Together, help the people in your group explore how they can commit to an intimate, genuine friendship with Jesus. Also help them see how they might go deeper with Jesus in response to his love and be more committed to the other friends in their lives.

Get-Together at a Glance

	WHAT PEOPLE WILL DO	MINUTES	SUPPLIES
CAFÉ TIME	Eat a snack or meal that connects with today's point. OPTIONS *(Choose One)*: ☐ *Quick and Easy:* Cinnamon Rolls ☐ *Easy Plus:* Orange Sticky Buns ☐ *High Impact:* Maple-Glazed Chicken	10 to 15 30 60	See pp. 187-188 for details
EXPERIENCING FRIENDSHIP	*The Search* Look for missing items and explore how God searches for and finds them.	10 to 12	• Bible
	Pulled Do an active experiment, then explore how Jesus' commitment to them leads to their commitment to him.	10 to 12	• 2 brooms • 9-foot rope • Bible
	Mixed Messages? Compare messages from the world and from God, and discuss how they might help encourage each other's commitment to God.	10 to 12	• newsprint or poster board • assortment of colored markers or crayons • 1 photocopy of "The Apostles' Creed" (p. 153) per person • Bibles • pens • sticky notes • *Friendship First* book per person
PRAYER	Write prayers to God and create a cross together.	5 to 10	• paper • pens or pencils
DAILY CHALLENGE	Talk about the Daily Challenges they'll carry out during the week.	up to 5	• *Friendship First* book per person • pens

Café Time

What friendship doesn't include eating together? Food is a very important part of the Friendship First experience. As we eat together, we grow closer together—we relax, we smile, we share. It's the perfect beginning to each friendship Get-Together. Remember that during these Get-Togethers, your focus is on people. Take the time to enjoy the fellowship of the table together.

We've provided three delicious options for each week's Get-Together. Choose the one that best fits your time, your setting, and your budget. See pages 187-188 for details on today's menu options.

Music IDEAS

Set a great atmosphere by playing background music that matches the mood of this Get-Together! Here are some genre suggestions:
- action film soundtrack
- country
- bluegrass
- rock

You can also play the Friendship First theme song, "Here for You" (track 11 on the *Friendship First* CD).

PURPOSE

Food that is sticky will lead to a discussion on true commitment in friendship.

☐ **QUICK AND EASY**
Cinnamon Rolls

or

☐ **EASY PLUS**
Orange Sticky Buns

or

☐ **HIGH IMPACT**
Maple-Glazed Chicken

HERE'S WHAT TO DO

- Make sure that each person feels welcome and at home at today's Get-Together. You may personally welcome each person, or if you'll be busy getting the last-minute details organized, find a warm, friendly person to be the greeter.

- If you're using the **Quick and Easy** or **Easy Plus** option, invite people to get a snack before they sit down in their groups of six.

- If you're using the **High Impact** option, wait until everyone's arrived, and ask the blessing.

- Have everyone fill a plate, sit down, and begin eating.

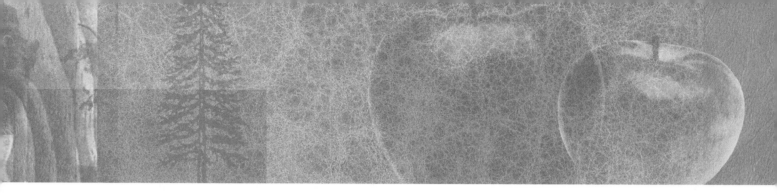

- While everyone's eating, allow for small talk and casual chatting.

- At some point in the conversation, discuss Chapter 6 in *Friendship First*. Ask people what struck them most from what they read.

- After a few minutes of discussion (or when there's a natural break in the conversation), discuss the significance of the food.

ASK **What could the food we're eating today symbolize about friendship? Let's think of as many possibilities as we can.**

SAY **Thanks for all your ideas! Our food today is sticky—it sticks to us. Today we're going to discuss how we can "stick" with others in friendship. We'll talk about Jesus' love and explore how we should be committed to God because God is committed to us.**

First let's check in on the Daily Challenges. How did you follow through with your Daily Challenge commitment? What happened as a result?

- Thank everyone for sharing a Daily Challenge story.

EXPERIENCING Friendship

The Search

Do this game to begin exploring how God is so committed to us that he "pursues" us, finds us, and treats us as valuable treasure.

HERE'S WHAT TO DO

- Have one volunteer leave the room.

- Hold a Bible, and announce that it represents all that is good.

- Ask the group to choose something that represents all that is evil. Gather ideas, and choose one based on a majority vote.

- Hide the Bible on one end or side of the room and hide the second object on the opposite end or side of the room.

- Tell people they are in one of two groups—those with birthdays in January through July will help the person find the Bible, and those with birthdays in August through December will help the person find the "evil" object.

- Tell both groups they'll help the person find the object by encouraging them with only these words: *hotter* and *colder*.

- Call the volunteer back in.

- For a few minutes, allow everyone else to give the volunteer "advice" about how close he or she is to the objects. It's entirely up to that person to choose who to listen to.

Searching for the "good!"

- Ask the volunteer:

  ASK **How did you feel?**

- Ask everyone else:

  ASK **How did you feel?**

- Discuss this question as a whole group:

  ASK **How is this experience like seeking God?**

- Read Matthew 13:45 aloud:

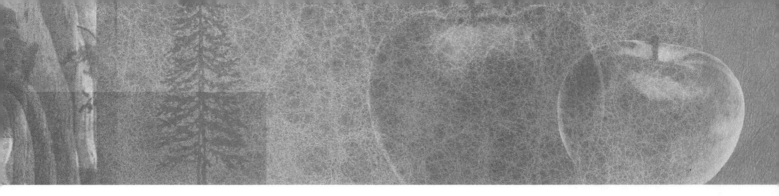

"Again, the Kingdom of Heaven is like a merchant on the lookout for choice pearls. When he discovered a pearl of great value, he sold everything he owned and bought it!"

- Discuss this question:

  ASK How does this metaphor illustrate the way God searches for us?

- Have people form pairs.

  SAY God searches for you like the merchant searches for a pearl. But God doesn't have distracting noise or messages—he hunts for you and finds you. Ezekiel 34:11-12 says, "For this is what the Sovereign Lord says: I myself will search and find my sheep. I will be like a shepherd looking for his scattered flock. I will find my sheep and rescue them from all the places where they were scattered on that dark and cloudy day."

- Have partners discuss these questions together:

  ASK When have you felt apart from God, like a lost sheep?

  How have you seen God's commitment to find and rescue you?

  How is a commitment to another person like or unlike a commitment to God?

> **INSIDE SCOOP** The teenagers in our group really got into this activity, and it ended up being a powerful metaphor for real life. Participants will probably draw a lot of comparisons between this experience and what it's like to make choices in their faith and relationships when they hear so many other "voices" distracting them from what's good.

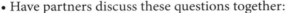

2 Pulled

Continue your discussion on the power of Christ's love and commitment to us with this object lesson.

HERE'S WHAT TO DO

- Have two people hold two brooms about 20 inches apart.

Pulling brooms together with a rope reveals what Jesus' love is like!

- Tie a 9-foot rope to one broom handle.

- Wrap the rope around the broom handles (about three times).

- Pull on the loose end of the rope as the volunteers try to keep the brooms apart. (For a more dramatic example, have two of the largest people hold the brooms while a smaller volunteer pulls the rope—but do *not* make size an issue!)

- The rope will pull the two brooms together no matter how hard the volunteers try to keep them apart.

- Get everyone involved in the broom activity. You can do the experiment a few more times with different people, or have multiple people holding the brooms apart while one person pulls on the rope.

- Afterward, read 2 Corinthians 5:14-15 aloud:

  "Either way, Christ's love controls us. Since we believe that Christ died for all, we also believe that we have all died to our old life. He died for everyone so that those who receive his new life will no longer live for themselves. Instead, they will live to please Christ, who died and was raised for them."

- Discuss this question:

  ASK How is what happened with the brooms like Jesus' love and commitment for us?

  SAY Just as the rope pulled the brooms together, God's love pulls us into friendship with Jesus and others. God's kindness leads us to repentance, and the more we fall in love with Jesus, the more we want to do things his way and share his love with others. It's all about Jesus' commitment, power, and strength—not ours. And, as we talked about earlier, our response to Jesus' love is automatic and natural. But sometimes people think responding to God's love *is* about our strength, and they are distracted by other messages about commitment.

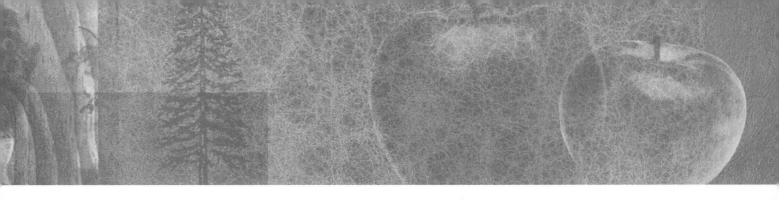

3 Mixed Messages?

In this Apostles' Creed activity, people will contrast human messages with God's messages.

HERE'S WHAT TO DO

- Place a large sheet of poster board or newsprint in the center of the room where everyone can see it.

- Have people write on the poster board or newsprint (using words, drawings, or symbols) human messages they have seen, heard, felt, or experienced. These could be slogans, attitudes, situations, images, pressures, or expectations.

- Next, give everyone a copy of "The Apostles' Creed" (p. 153).

- Explain that in the early days of Christianity, the young church wanted to come up with a statement that would express and remind them of what they believed. The Apostles' Creed was developed between the second and ninth centuries and was used often as a confession for baptism, which was a time when many identified themselves as Christians.

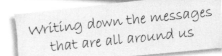

Writing down the messages that are all around us

- Read the creed aloud together.

- Ask everyone to return to the poster board or newsprint to write statements, words, drawings, or symbols of messages—based on what they read—from God. These new ideas can be written anywhere on the paper, mixed with the other statements.

- Discuss these questions:

  ASK When you look at this (the poster board or newsprint), **what feelings or thoughts do you have?**

  What can we discover about God's commitment to us?

  How can we be committed to God and others in a world with so many mixed messages?

- Have people form pairs, and have pairs discuss this question:

  ASK Finish this sentence. "You can help me listen to the right messages from God by…"

12

Stick with Jesus and others.

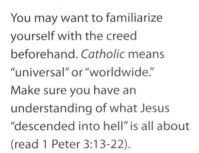

Between Friends

You may want to familiarize yourself with the creed beforehand. *Catholic* means "universal" or "worldwide." Make sure you have an understanding of what Jesus "descended into hell" is all about (read 1 Peter 3:13-22).

- After pairs share ideas, have everyone write on a sticky note one way he or she will commit to listen to God's messages or help friends listen to God's messages.

- Have people stick their notes on the poster board or newsprint as they explain to the group what they will do to "stick to" God's messages and be a committed friend to Jesus and others.

- Have people return to their pairs.

- Have pairs go to page 123 of *Friendship First* and read together the "Friendship First" section.

- Partners should discuss their thoughts and feelings about this box and their answers to the question, "Are you committed to God?"

- After a couple minutes, have pairs do an affirmation activity.

- Ask partners to tell each other what they appreciate about the other's commitment in friendship—either with Jesus or with others. They can name a quality or characteristic that makes the person someone who "sticks with" a friend.

- Allow a minute for partners to encourage each other.

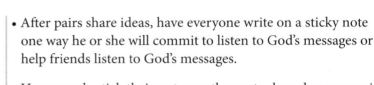

FOR DEEPER IMPACT

You may also include Matthew 13:24-30 in this experience. Read aloud the following, and then discuss what the passage shows us about God's love, purposes, and commitment.

> **Here is another story Jesus told: "The Kingdom of Heaven is like a farmer who planted good seed in his field. But that night as the workers slept, his enemy came and planted weeds among the wheat, then slipped away. When the crop began to grow and produce grain, the weeds also appeared.**
>
> **"The farmer's workers went to him and said, 'Sir, the field where you planted that good seed is full of weeds! Where did they come from?'**

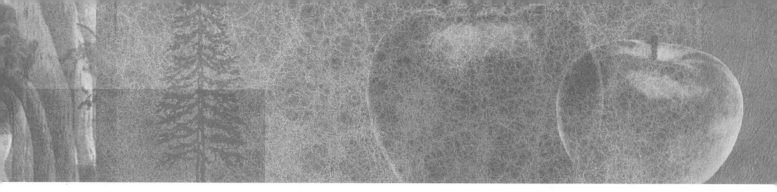

" 'An enemy has done this!' the farmer exclaimed.

" 'Should we pull out the weeds?' they asked.

" 'No,' he replied, 'you'll uproot the wheat if you do. Let both grow together until the harvest. Then I will tell the harvesters to sort out the weeds, tie them into bundles, and burn them, and to put the wheat in the barn.' " (Matthew 13:24-30).

FOR DEEPER IMPACT

Read 2 Corinthians 5:14-15 again, and discuss what this passage tells us about Jesus' amazing love. Talk about how the entire Bible is a love letter from God to us. Consider together what a love letter includes, and discuss its impact on the person who receives it. How do we feel about and respond to a love letter from God?

The Apostles' Creed

I believe in God, the Father Almighty,

    the Creator of heaven and earth,

    and in Jesus Christ, His only Son, our Lord:

Who was conceived of the Holy Spirit,

    born of the Virgin Mary,

    suffered under Pontius Pilate,

    was crucified, died, and was buried.

He descended into hell.

The third day He arose again from the dead.

He ascended into heaven

    and sits at the right hand of God the Father Almighty,

    whence He shall come to judge the living and the dead.

I believe in the Holy Spirit, the holy catholic church,

    the communion of saints,

    the forgiveness of sins,

    the resurrection of the body,

    and life everlasting.

Amen.

Prayer

In this creative prayer experience, people will express their prayers of commitment and work together to build a cross.

HERE'S WHAT TO DO

- Have the group form a circle.

- Provide paper and pens, and have everyone write a prayer about friendship commitment. The prayer could ask God for help to respond to his committed love and grace, confess a struggle or fear, or express the desire to listen only to God's messages and commit to them above all others.

- Ask people to tear the paper into the shape of a cross and hold it to their chest, giving the prayer quietly and personally to God.

- After about 20 seconds, have people set the crosses in the center of the circle and work together to make one big cross.

- Using this symbol of Jesus' love as the focus, pray aloud in closing.

PRAY **Jesus, your love brings us to you. Your kindness brings us to repentance. Your commitment to us leads us to glorify you. It's what you've made us for. Thanks for lavishing love, kindness, and grace upon us. Thank you for searching for us and finding us. Help us grow deeper in a friendship with you, our best friend, and help us commit to sticking with others in friendship. Amen.**

- Explain that the group will exchange small gifts during the next Get-Together. (You may want to set limits. For example, the gift must cost less than three dollars, the gifts can only be care cards, or they must be homemade.)

- Have people write their name on a slip of paper, and set all the slips of paper upside down in a pile.

- Have everyone draw the name of the person he or she will present a thoughtful gift to next time.

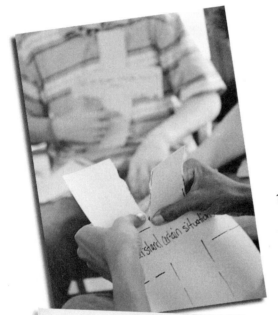

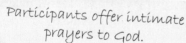

Participants offer intimate prayers to God.

Daily Challenge™

The Daily Challenge will give people an opportunity to practice what they explored during the week's Get-Together.

HERE'S WHAT TO DO

- Have everyone go to page 138 of *Friendship First*. Have a volunteer read the "Stick With Jesus and Others" Daily Challenges aloud.

- Have everyone choose one of the challenges to do in the coming week and mark it in the book. Ask people to take turns around the room telling which challenge they plan to do.

- Have each person choose and take home a sticky note from the "Mixed Messages?" activity that represents his or her commitment to help others better listen to God's message. This note will be a tangible reminder to follow through on the Daily Challenge.

- Tell everyone to be ready to report on how the Daily Challenge went next time the group meets.

- Encourage everyone to continue reading Chapter 7 of *Friendship First* throughout the week.

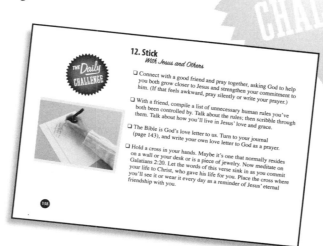

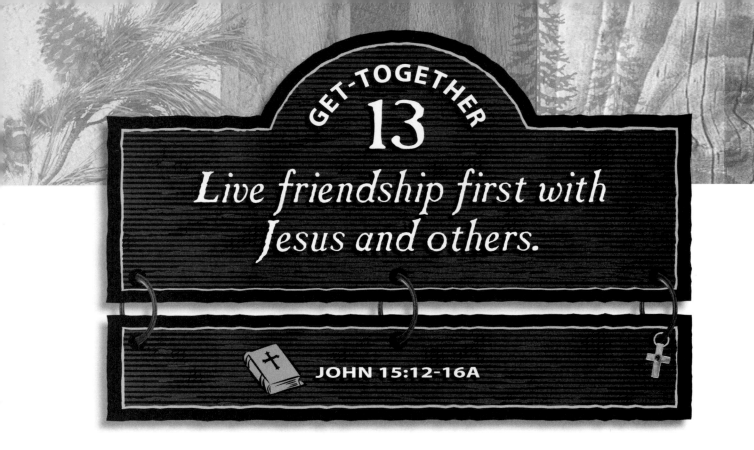

GET-TOGETHER

13

Live friendship first with Jesus and others.

JOHN 15:12-16A

Being friends with Jesus is an incredible, lifelong adventure. When we're open to his leading, Jesus will send us places we never dreamed of to serve, love, and care for others in unimaginable ways! What a privilege we have to serve our best friend, Jesus, every day of our lives. We've been chosen by God—hand-picked to share Jesus' love wherever we go, whatever we do. This is what we were born for. Our Best Friend wants us to go throughout the world befriending others in his name. Sounds fun, doesn't it! Let's not waste another moment!

Get-Together at a Glance

CAFÉ TIME

EXPERIENCING FRIENDSHIP

PRAYER

DAILY CHALLENGE

WHAT PEOPLE WILL DO	MINUTES	SUPPLIES
Eat a snack or meal that connects with today's point. OPTIONS *(Choose One)*:		See pp. 189-190 for details
☐ *Quick and Easy:* Fresh Fruit Trays	10 to 15	
☐ *Easy Plus:* Fruit Smoothies	30	
☐ *High Impact:* Grilled Chicken and Pineapple Sandwiches	60	

Friendship Celebration and Review

Exchange gifts, and talk about what they've learned.	10 to 12	• *Friendship First* CD • CD player

Friendship Town

Create a friendly town and talk about the difference being friends with Jesus can make.	10 to 12	• poster board • markers in a variety of colors • scissors

The 1 Thing Revisited

Consider new insights into the Mary and Martha story.	10 to 12	• Bible • 1 Thing pins—order at www.friendshipfirst.com

Optional Commissioning Activity

		• *Friendship First* DVD • DVD player and TV

Look at John 15:9-16, pray about how to live Friendship First and begin sharing God's love with others.	5 to 10	• Bible per person

Talk about the Daily Challenges.	up to 5	• *Friendship First* book per person 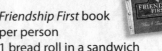 • 1 bread roll in a sandwich bag per person

Café Time

What friendship doesn't include eating together? Food is a very important part of the Friendship First experience. As we eat together, we grow closer together—we relax, we smile, we share. It's the perfect beginning to each friendship Get-Together. Remember that during these Get-Togethers, your focus is on people. Take the time to enjoy the fellowship of the table together.

We've provided three delicious options for each week's Get-Together. Choose the one that best fits your time, your setting, and your budget. See pages 189-190 for details on today's menu options.

PURPOSE

In today's Get-Together, participants will explore the fruitfulness of friendship. All of today's food has a fruity theme.

☐ **QUICK AND EASY**
Fresh Fruit Trays

or

☐ **EASY PLUS**
Fruit Smoothies

or

☐ **HIGH IMPACT**
Grilled Chicken and Pineapple Sandwiches

HERE'S WHAT TO DO

- Make sure that each person feels welcome and at home at today's Get-Together. You may personally welcome each person, or if you'll be busy getting the last-minute details organized, find a warm, friendly person to be the greeter.

- If you're using the **Quick and Easy** or **Easy Plus** option, invite people to get a snack before they sit down in their groups of six. Then continue with the discussion below.

- If you're using the **High Impact** option, wait until everyone has arrived.

- Ask the blessing.

- Have everyone fill a plate, sit down, and begin eating.

Music IDEAS

Set a great atmosphere by playing background music that matches the mood of this Get-Together! Here are some genre suggestions:

- upbeat praise
- reggae
- fun pop music

You can also play the Friendship First theme song, "Here for You" (track 11 on the *Friendship First* CD).

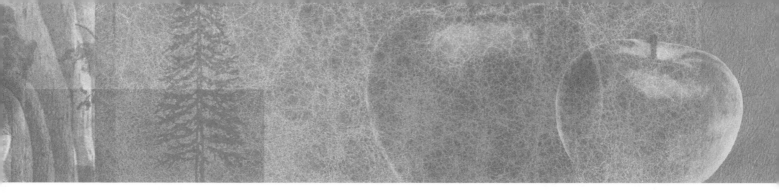

- While everyone's eating, allow for small talk and casual chatting.

- At some point in the conversation, discuss Chapter 7 in *Friendship First*. Ask people what struck them most from what they read.

- After a few minutes of discussion (or when there's a natural break in the conversation), discuss the significance of the food.

ASK **What could the food we're eating today symbolize about friendship? Let's think of as many possibilities as we can.**

SAY **These are all great insights into friendship. Our meal today included lots of fruit. Today we'll be talking about the fruitfulness of friendship. We'll also discover that God wants us to produce fruit that lasts.**

Now let's check in on the Daily Challenges. How did you follow through with your Daily Challenge commitment and what happened as a result?

- Thank everyone for sharing a Daily Challenge story.

EXPERIENCING
Friendship

A gift exchange is an affirming, fun experience for all.

INSIDE SCOOP The gift-giving experience was a very meaningful and emotional time for our participants. You might be tempted to skip it because it does require a commitment from each person to take time to choose a gift and to spend a bit of money on it. Please don't skip this activity. It was a wonderful time of affirmation for each person, and all of the gifts were thoughtful and creative.

INSIDE SCOOP There's lots of activities in today's Get-Together. Exchanging gifts can take quite a while. Watch time carefully during this activity and do all you can to keep things moving along.

Friendship Celebration and Review

This activity will help participants celebrate the friendships they've developed over the last 12 weeks.

HERE'S WHAT TO DO

SAY Today is a celebration of friendship. Let's begin our celebration by exchanging gifts with our friends!

• Play "Joy to the World," track 10 on the *Friendship First* CD.

• Have people take turns exchanging gifts.

• Have people tell why they chose the gift they brought.

SAY These weeks have been wonderful—we're much better friends than we were at the beginning. It feels great to celebrate this experience with all of you.

• Discuss this question:

ASK Why do you think God has put our group together for these weeks?

SAY I am so glad that we have been together during these weeks as we gathered to talk about becoming better friends with one another and with God. I have learned so much about friendship from each of you. Today, let's explore where we're going to go from here.

Friendship Town

In this activity, participants will think about what their community could be like if people were real friends with one another and with God.

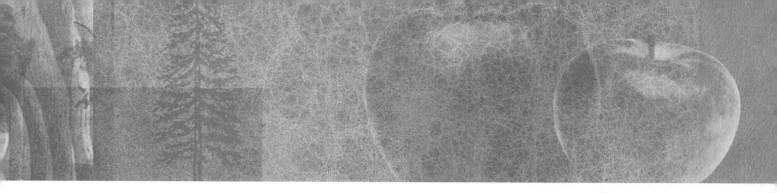

HERE'S WHAT TO DO

- Before the Get-Together, gather one large sheet of poster board for every six to eight people. You could also use butcher paper or newsprint.

- Cut the poster board into sixths. In small print, write one of the following places on each of the poster board pieces: workplaces, parks, courthouses, markets/stores, neighborhoods, schools.

- Gather markers in an assortment of colors.

- Form pairs or trios—you'll need three small groups for each group of six to eight.

- Give each pair or trio two sections of the poster board and one marker.

  SAY **Each group has been given a couple of small pieces of the larger community. With your partner(s), talk about what your pieces of the community would look like if everyone lived according to the friendship principles we've talked about during the last 12 weeks. Draw your section of the town and include visual symbols of your ideas of what the community would look like.**

- Give the groups no more than three minutes to talk and draw.

  SAY **Now revisit your pieces of the community and talk about what our community would be like if everyone became an intimate friend of God. Here is a specific question to consider:**

  ASK **How are our lives changed if we believe that God is a friend who wants to be actively involved in each and every part of life?**

  SAY **Use a different colored marker to write or draw your ideas on your poster board.**

- Hand out different colored markers to each small group.

Transform your community with the power of friendship!

- Give groups no more than three minutes to talk and write.

- Get everyone's attention, and have each pair or trio share its sections of the community with everyone else. Discuss how friendship with Jesus changes our lives.

ASK How is celebrating and living friendship with others like celebrating and living a friendship with God?

The 1 Thing Revisited

In this activity, participants will consider new insights into the Mary and Martha story.

HERE'S WHAT TO DO

SAY During our first Get-Together, we explored Luke 10:38-42. Let me read it to you one more time:

"As Jesus and the disciples continued on their way to Jerusalem, they came to a certain village where a woman named Martha welcomed them into her home. Her sister, Mary, sat at the Lord's feet, listening to what he taught. But Martha was distracted by the big dinner she was preparing. She came to Jesus and said, 'Lord, doesn't it seem unfair to you that my sister just sits here while I do all the work? Tell her to come and help me.'

"But the Lord said to her, 'My dear Martha, you are worried and upset over all these details! There is really only one thing worth being concerned about. Mary has discovered it, and it will not be taken away from her.' "

- Discuss this question:

ASK What insights about this passage do you have now after exploring friendship with this group?

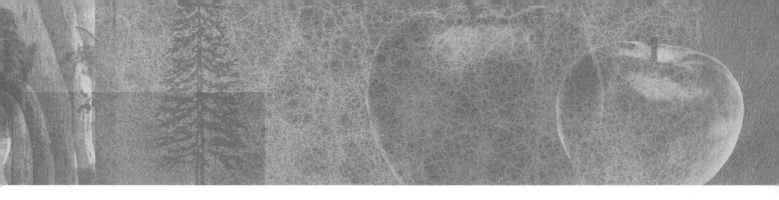

SAY Mary was concerned about Jesus and her relationship with him. Our friendship with Jesus is our number one priority. When we put Jesus first, we will lead purposeful, meaningful, abundant lives. I'd like to give you a reminder to put friendship with Jesus first.

- Give each person a "1 Thing" pin and, as you do, bless or pray for that person. For example, you might say, "May God bless you as you put him first daily." Or you might pray, "Dear God, please encourage Brian to seek you with his whole heart each day."

Optional Commissioning Activity

You may want to remind your Friendship First participants of all the things you've covered during these 13 Get-Togethers. Here's a great activity to help you do that.

HERE'S WHAT TO DO

- Cue the *Friendship First* DVD to the segment titled "Commissioning."

  SAY We've talked about so many aspects of friendship during these weeks. Let's watch this DVD segment and remember our time together.

- Show the DVD segment.

- Discuss this question:

  ASK What do you think were the highlights of our time together?

  How has this DVD segment inspired you to live friendship first?

Participants are reminded of what they've learned and are commissioned to be friends to others.

Prayer

HERE'S WHAT TO DO

SAY **The night before Jesus was crucified, he met with his disciples to celebrate the Passover. During that evening he had many things to say to his disciples.**

Just imagine how he must have felt. He knew what would happen the next day. He knew this was his last opportunity to teach and encourage his best friends. His words were passionate and urgent. Let's read aloud a portion of what Jesus said to his disciples.

• Have everyone turn to John 15:9-16 in his or her Bible, and have one person read aloud while everyone else follows along.

• Discuss this question:

ASK **What lessons can we glean from these words about how we're to live our lives?**

SAY **Today is our last meeting. While there is a sense of celebration because of all we've shared with each other, there is also a sense of urgency. God has chosen us! And he wants us to love others passionately and to produce lasting fruit.**

• Have everyone pray silently about how Jesus wants them to follow his words of instruction. Invite the group to write their ideas on the fruit shapes on page 124 of *Friendship First*.

• Close the prayer time.

• Hold up a bread roll.

SAY **As we end this series of Get-Togethers, it's time to consider what happens next. Scripture tells us that Jesus Christ is the bread of life. We're to share him—his grace, his love, his friendship—with everyone we encounter. Let's share him right now.**

• Take a small pinch of the roll. Hand the rest of the roll to the person on your right, and complete this sentence, "[Person's name], I'd like to share Jesus' _____ with you right now." You might fill in the blank with the word "peace" or "love."

Share Jesus' grace, love, and friendship with others. There's always enough for everyone.

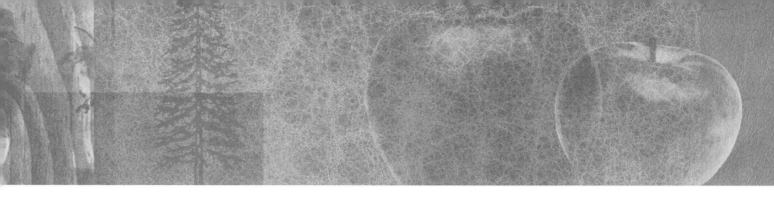

- Have people take turns around the room pinching a piece of the roll for themselves, handing the roll to the next person, and completing the sentence.

- When the remains of the roll return to you, discuss these questions:

  ASK **What were you thinking and feeling during this activity?**

  What discoveries did you make during this activity?

  SAY **There is always enough of Jesus to go around! His love and grace are available to all. And as Jesus' good friends, we have the privilege of sharing his love with others and inviting them to be Jesus' friends too. Let's end our time with prayer!**

- Close the session in prayer, asking God to bless each member of the group as they seek to be better friends with others and with God.

Between Friends

You may want to plan a Friendship First reunion. Get together in a few weeks for a picnic, a potluck, a holiday party, or some other fun get-together.

Today's Daily Challenge will give each person an opportunity to practice what they've explored in each week's Get-Together. The group will also be given an opportunity to consider what they'd like to do next.

HERE'S WHAT TO DO

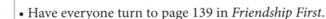

- Have everyone turn to page 139 in *Friendship First.*

- Read the "Live Friendship First" Daily Challenges together and decide what you'd like to do next.

- Give each person a bread roll in a plastic baggie as a reminder to share the love of Jesus with others and do the Daily Challenges.

Pointers for the Café Time Coordinator

Here are some ideas to help make the Café Time section of each Friendship First Get-Together easy, fun, and meaningful.

• Share the fun! Find several cooks who can share the shopping, cooking, and hosting. Sign them up ahead of time, and give them all the information they'll need upfront. They'll need to have the recipes. They'll also need to know where the Get-Together will be; what they need to provide other than the food, such as paper goods and decorations; and how to handle the finances.

• If you're meeting in homes, consider rotating from home to home, and have each home host prepare the meal or snack for that week.

• If you're meeting at the church, be sure that your cooks have access to the kitchen and know all about your church's kitchen procedures.

• Call each cook a week ahead of time to make sure they've got everything they need. Make sure the cooks have your phone number or e-mail address so they can get in contact with you if they have problems or questions.

• Contact the Get-Together leader frequently to touch base and make sure that you are each aware of the other's plans.

• Understand how important the food is to each Get-Together. The food for each week is specially planned to tie in to the theme of the Get-Together. It's the highlight of the meeting! You'll find the purpose for the food at the top of each page of recipes. Be sure the cooks understand how important their role is in helping the participants learn more about friendship with others and with Jesus.

• Make sure to make a plan for paying for the food. You may want to have the church pay for it all. If so, make sure the cooks all know to keep track of their receipts. Or you may want to have each participant pay a small amount each week. If the meetings rotate from house to house, you may want to have each host pay for the food that he or she prepares.

• You may also want to line up helpers to set up the tables and chairs, set the tables, and help with the clean-up.

• Even if you decide to go with the snack options, plan to serve a meal at a few of the Get-Togethers. There's something especially warm and intimate about sharing a meal together with friends.

• Pray for each cook and the participants at each Get-Together. Ask God to bless your efforts and use them for his glory as people learn how to be better friends with others and with Jesus.

• Have fun!

Pointers for the Café Time Cooks

• Understand how important the food is to each Get-Together. The food for each week is specially planned to tie in to the theme of the Get-Together. It's the highlight of the meeting! You'll find the purpose for the food at the top of each page of recipes. Be sure the cooks understand how important their role is in helping the participants learn more about friendship with others and with Jesus.

• Make sure you get all the information you need from the Café Time coordinator. You'll need to have the recipes, and you'll need to know where the Get-Together will be held. You'll also need to know if you need to provide anything other than the food (for example, serving bowls, tablecloths, paper goods).

• Be sure you know how to handle the cost. Keep your receipts if the church will be reimbursing you.

• Talk to the Café Time coordinator about finding helpers for kitchen and clean-up duties.

• Be sure to keep the specifics of each week's menu secret. Part of the fun of the Get-Together is the surprise of the food each week. Keep the food under wraps in the kitchen until it's time to serve.

• Pray for the Café Time coordinator and the participants at each Get-Together. Ask God to bless your efforts and use them for his glory as people learn how to be better friends with others and with Jesus.

• Have fun!

GET-TOGETHER 1

Make friendship a priority with Jesus and others.

FOOD CONNECTION

People will find a variety of ingredients in their snack or meal today. Each ingredient offers something unique to the taste. In the same way, each person brings something unique to the Friendship First group of friends.

Don't forget the paper goods!

Bring:

☐ plates

☐ bowls

☐ cups

☐ flatware

☐ napkins

as needed.

■ Quick and Easy MENU

- trail mix
- beverages

Purchase several varieties of store-bought trail mix, snack mix, or granola (1/2 cup to 1 cup per person). Pour the trail mix into large serving bowls, put large spoons or scoops in the bowls, and place the bowls on a serving table with beverages. Put disposable cups and napkins nearby.

■ Easy Plus MENU

- ice-cream-sundae bar*
- beverages

Purchase several varieties of ice cream, as well as toppings, fruit, candies, nuts, and whipped cream. Set everything out on a table with bowls, spoons, ice-cream scoops, and napkins. Have everyone create his or her own ice-cream sundae.

* Getting together in the morning? You can easily adapt this to a yogurt and fruit bar. Provide yogurt and a variety of fruit and granola toppings.

■ High Impact MENU

- salad bar
- french bread and butter
- crackers
- cookies
- beverages

Salad Bar

Set up a salad bar with a variety of ingredients, including:

Veggies, chopped, sliced, or grated as needed (carrots, tomatoes, cucumbers, green peppers, mushrooms, canned beets, zucchini, radishes, green onions, olives, jicama, celery, kidney beans, garbanzo beans, corn, or peas)

shredded cheeses (cheddar, swiss, or pepper jack)

diced ham or turkey

chopped eggs

crunchy toppings (sunflower seeds, bacon bits, fish crackers, and croutons)

variety of salad dressings (Plan on a third to half a cup per person.)

SERVING TIPS

If you're meeting with several Friendship First groups, set up the salad bar on a long table so that people can form two lines. They'll serve themselves more quickly and have more time to chat and get to know each other.

GET-TOGETHER 2

Go beyond first impressions with Jesus and others.

FOOD CONNECTION

Today's Get-Together talks about our first impressions and our misconceptions about God. In each of the food options, there's something people won't expect based on the food's appearance. Today's food will help the participants talk about how our first impressions are not always accurate.

Don't forget the paper goods!

Bring:

- ☐ plates
- ☐ bowls
- ☐ cups
- ☐ flatware
- ☐ napkins

as needed.

■ Quick and Easy MENU

- cornflakes with colored milk
- beverages

Purchase cornflakes and milk in paper cartons. Pour the milk into a large pitcher, and tint it green or blue with liquid food coloring. Pour the milk back into the milk carton so people won't see that it's tinted until they pour it onto their cereal. Surprise!

■ Easy Plus MENU

- gelatin "drinks"
- beverages

Gelatin Drinks

1 small package of red Jell-O for every two people
clear plastic glasses
straws

Prepare the Jell-O according to the package directions. Make the preparations go faster by preparing all the Jell-O at once in one big bowl. Then pour it into the glasses. Place a straw in each glass. Place on a tray in the refrigerator for several hours. Serve the "drinks." Once everyone has noticed that they aren't really drinks, provide spoons and beverages.

■ High Impact MENU

- meatloaf cake
- tossed salad
- french bread with butter
- beverages
- cookies

Meatloaf Cake *(serves 10 to 12)*

Meatloaf:
3 pounds lean ground beef (90 percent lean,
    or more if possible)
1 large onion, finely chopped
2 carrots, finely shredded
1 green pepper, finely chopped
1 sleeve saltine crackers, finely crushed
3 eggs
2/3 cup ketchup
2 teaspoons salt
1 teaspoon pepper

Mashed potatoes:
4 pounds potatoes
1/2 cup butter
1 teaspoon salt
up to 1 cup milk

Mix all the meatloaf ingredients well. Divide the mixture, and pack into two 8-inch round cake pans. Flatten the top of the meat mixture. Bake at 375° F for one hour.

Meanwhile, scrub, peel, and boil the potatoes until tender. Drain well. Then mash the potatoes, adding the butter and salt. Using an electric mixer, whip the potatoes until no lumps remain, adding only enough milk to create a stiff but spreadable mixture. Set aside and keep warm.

Remove the meatloaf layers from the oven. One by one, press the cooked meatloaves with a wide spatula and tilt the pans slightly over a bowl to drain off the grease. Carefully remove one meatloaf from the pan, and place it on a serving platter. Put about a cup or so of stiff, fluffy mashed potatoes on top, and gently spread the potatoes to the edges. Remove the other meatloaf from the pan, and gently place it on top of the first meatloaf. Spread mashed potatoes on the top and sides of the meatloaf as you would a layer cake. Place the remaining mashed potatoes into a pastry bag fitted with a large star or shell tip (you may need to add a bit more milk so the potatoes will pipe well). You can also use a reclosable freezer bag with a coupler and a tip. Make a shell border or small stars around the top and bottom

edge of the mashed potato cake. Garnish with cherry tomatoes and green onion "leaves," if desired.

An easier option would be to purchase already-made meatloaf and mashed potatoes from the grocery store or from a restaurant such as Boston Market. Continue with the decorating instructions.

Tossed Salad
Make your favorite tossed salad. Serve with a variety of dressings.

French Bread
Purchase a loaf of french bread. Slice the loaf, and butter each slice. Wrap the sliced loaf in aluminum foil, and bake at 350° F for 15 to 20 minutes to melt the butter.

Cookies
Serve your favorite homemade or store-bought cookies.

*Experience
love
with Jesus
and others.*

FOOD CONNECTION

Today's Get-Together talks about love, and all the food has a valentine theme.

■ Quick and Easy MENU

- heart-shaped cookies
- beverages

Purchase heart-shaped cookies from a local bakery or grocery store.

■ Easy Plus MENU

- heart-shaped muffins
- beverages

Heart-Shaped Muffins *(makes 12)*

2 cups flour
3 teaspoons baking powder
1/2 teaspoon salt
1/2 cup sugar

1 egg, slightly beaten
1 cup milk
1/4 cup melted butter
1 cup fresh or frozen raspberries

Place foil liners in a muffin tin. Preheat the oven to 400° F. Sift 1 3/4 cups flour, baking powder, salt, and sugar into a mixing bowl. In another bowl, stir together the egg, milk, and butter. Gently stir the two mixtures together just until all the flour is incorporated. Sprinkle the remaining 1/4 cup of flour over 1 cup of raspberries. Gently fold the raspberries into the batter. Spoon batter into each foil muffin liner so it's two-thirds full. Place a marble between the foil liner and the muffin tin. Bake about 15 minutes.

Note: If you don't have marbles, simply frost the muffins and use red candies to form a heart on top of each muffin.

Frosting: Beat 3 ounces softened cream cheese, 1 tablespoon warm water, 1 teaspoon vanilla extract, and 3 cups sifted powdered sugar until smooth. Tint the frosting pink by adding one or two drops of red food coloring.

*Don't forget the
paper goods!*

Bring:

- ☐ plates
- ☐ bowls
- ☐ cups
- ☐ flatware
- ☐ napkins

as needed.

■ High Impact MENU

- heart-shaped pizza
- heart-beet salad
- heart cake
- beverages

Heart-Shaped Pizza

(makes 2 pizzas, each serves 4)

1 to 1 1/2 cup warm water

2 tablespoons dry yeast (or two packages)

2 teaspoons sugar

4 cups flour

2 tablespoons olive oil

1 teaspoon salt

2 teaspoons Italian seasoning

pizza sauce

cheese

pizza toppings

Combine 1/2 cup of the water with the yeast and sugar. Stir until yeast is dissolved. Wait about 5 minutes until the mixture is foamy. Add the flour, oil, salt, and Italian seasoning. Stir in enough of the remaining water to moisten all the flour and make a dough. Knead the dough for three or four minutes, adding in flour as needed if the dough is sticky. Place in a greased bowl, cover with a dampened towel, and let rise 30 minutes.

Preheat the oven to 450° F. Lightly grease 2 pizza pans. Divide the dough in half. Pat out each mound of dough into a large heart shape. Top each pizza crust with your favorite brand of pizza or spaghetti sauce, pepperoni (or other pizza toppings), 2 cups mozzarella cheese, and 1/2 cup parmesan cheese. Bake for 15 to 20 minutes or until the crust is golden brown and the cheese is melted. Halfway through the baking time, reverse the pizzas' position in the oven. Let the pizzas sit 5 minutes before slicing.

An easier option would be to top a frozen grocery store pizza with heart-shaped pepperoni. Simply use scissors to cut each slice of pepperoni into a heart shape. Or ask a pizza restaurant (such as Papa Murphy's) if they will make a heart-shaped pizza.

Heart-Beet Salad

Use a small heart-shaped cookie cutter to cut canned beets into heart shapes. Dry the beets with a paper towel. Add to your favorite salad vegetables, and toss with Italian dressing.

Heart Cake

Bake a pink cake using a store-bought mix. Cool completely. Frost with purchased pink frosting. Use red candies and red decorator sugar to form a large heart shape on top of the cake.

Find unconditional acceptance with Jesus and others.

FOOD CONNECTION

In each of today's food options, there is something unusual that doesn't seem to belong. This will help the Friendship First friends talk about feeling that they don't belong and the unconditional acceptance that Jesus offers us and that we can offer to others.

Don't forget the paper goods!

Bring:

- ☐ plates
- ☐ bowls
- ☐ cups
- ☐ flatware
- ☐ napkins

as needed.

■ Quick and Easy MENU

- bagels and toppings
- beverages

Purchase a variety of bagels and toppings. Toppings might include flavored cream cheeses, jams, and jellies. Include some unusual toppings such as hummus, goat cheese, peanut butter, Nutella (a cocoa and hazelnut spread), and cake frosting. Set out sharp knives and cutting boards. You may want to provide a toaster, too.

■ Easy Plus MENU

- beverages
- chocolate zucchini cake

Chocolate Zucchini Cake *(serves 12)*

2 1/2 cups flour	2 cups sugar
1/2 cup cocoa	3 eggs
2 1/2 teaspoons baking powder	1 teaspoon vanilla
1 1/2 teaspoons baking soda	1/2 cup milk
1 teaspoon cinnamon	2 cup shredded zucchini
1/2 teaspoon salt	1 cup chopped walnuts or pecans
3/4 cup butter or margarine	1 cup chocolate chips

Preheat oven to 350º F. Combine all the dry ingredients except the sugar. In another bowl, cream the sugar and butter until fluffy. Beat in one egg at a time. Stir in vanilla. Add dry ingredients alternating with milk. Stir in the zucchini and nuts. Pour into greased and floured 9x13 cake pan. Sprinkle chocolate chips on top. Bake 50 to 60 minutes until cake tests done.

■ High Impact MENU

• gourmet fast food

Set the table with your nicest linens, china, crystal, and silverware. If you don't own nice china, find some you can borrow from or try your local rental store. Provide fresh flowers for a centerpiece.

Pour soda into nice pitchers, and keep the pitchers in the refrigerator. Purchase plain hamburgers, cheeseburgers, and french fries from your favorite fast-food restaurant. Put the food on platters, and keep the platters warm in the oven until the group is seated and the blessing has been asked. Then bring out the pitchers of soda and the platters of fast food and serve each person.

SERVING TIPS:

It's very important that no one sees the food beforehand. The participants should only see an elegantly set table. Don't give anyone any clues about what the food is or isn't—the surprise of serving plain fast-food hamburgers on china will make a huge impact on the group.

Also, make sure the centerpieces are low so that the participants can see each other across the table.

GET-TOGETHER 5

Listen to Jesus and others.

FOOD CONNECTION

Today's Get-Together is all about listening—so all of the food is noisy and crunchy. It'll help the group talk about things that distract them from listening.

■ Quick and Easy MENU

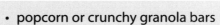

- popcorn or crunchy granola bars
- beverages

Purchase bags of already popped, flavored popcorn or a variety of crunchy granola bars.

■ Easy Plus MENU

- tortilla chips and dip
- beverages

Purchase a bag of flour tortillas. Cut each of the tortillas into six to eight wedges. Place on a baking sheet and bake at 400° F until crispy and light brown. Serve warm with your favorite marinara sauce.

An easier option would be to simply buy a bag of tortilla chips and serve with your favorite salsa.

Don't forget the paper goods!

Bring:

☐ plates
☐ bowls
☐ cups
☐ flatware
☐ napkins

as needed.

■ High Impact MENU

- Fritos pie
- carrot and celery sticks
- beverages
- Key lime pie

Fritos Pie *(serves 4 to 6)*

2 pounds ground beef

8-ounce can tomato sauce

6-ounce can tomato paste

16-ounce can stewed tomatoes

2 tablespoons chili powder

1 1/2 teaspoons salt

1 teaspoon hot pepper sauce (more or less, depending on taste)

1 or 2 individual bags of Fritos corn chips for each person

2 pounds cheddar cheese, shredded

1 large onion, finely chopped onion

Individual bags of Fritos corn chips

Brown the beef. Drain. Combine all ingredients (except the chips) in a large pot and simmer for at least an hour. Or cook in a slow cooker on low for 8 to 10 hours. Taste and adjust seasonings before serving.

Have everyone pour a bag of Fritos corn chips into a bowl and ladle chili on top of the Fritos. Top with cheese and onions if desired.

An easier option would be to purchase canned chili for the Fritos pie.

Key Lime Pie

(makes 2 pies, each serves 6)

1 can sweetened condensed milk

8 ounces cream cheese, softened

1/2 cup Key lime juice (or fresh lime juice)

12-ounce tub of Cool Whip whipped topping, thawed

2 store-bought graham-cracker crusts.

Use a hand mixer to blend the milk and cheese until smooth. Add the lime juice, and mix thoroughly. Gently fold in the thawed Cool Whip. Add a drop or two of green food coloring if desired. Pour into the pie shells. Refrigerate 6 hours before serving.

Find comfort in Jesus and others.

FOOD CONNECTION

Today's Get-Together is about finding comfort in Jesus despite our brokenness and imperfections. Jesus can take our troubled, broken lives and create something beautiful! All of today's food includes some kind of "breaking."

Don't forget the paper goods!

Bring:

☐ plates
☐ bowls
☐ cups
☐ flatware
☐ napkins

as needed.

■ Quick and Easy MENU

- peanut brittle
- beverages

Purchase peanut brittle to serve. Invite each person to break off several pieces of the peanut brittle to eat.

■ Easy Plus MENU

- broken glass dessert
- beverages

Broken Glass Dessert *(serves 16)*

5 small packages of different colors of Jell-O gelatin
1 large package of lemon Jell-O
1 large tub Cool Whip whipped topping
6 graham crackers (large rectangular sheets)
1/2 cup sugar
6 tablespoons butter or margarine

At least 24 hours before serving, prepare each of the five packages of Jell-O separately, using 1 1/2 cups boiling water per package. Refrigerate several hours until set. When set, cut the gelatin into cubes, and put the cubes in a 9x12 glass pan. Mix the large package of lemon Jell-O with 2 cups of boiling water. Cool to room temperature. Gently fold the lemon Jell-O into the Cool Whip. Pour onto the cubed gelatin. Use a spatula to push the Cool Whip mixture between the Jell-O cubes and spread it on top. Crush the graham crackers in a food processor and mix them with sugar. Toss the crumbs with melted butter or margarine, and sprinkle the graham cracker crumbs on top of the Cool Whip. Refrigerate for at least 6 or 7 hours to set. Cut into squares to serve.

■ High Impact MENU

- crunchy chicken salad
- rolls and butter
- beverages
- cookies

Crunchy Chicken Salad

(makes 8 to 10 generous servings)

Salad:

One 16-ounce package three-color deli coleslaw
(mixture of green cabbage, carrots, and red
cabbage)

two 16-ounce packages broccoli coleslaw (mixture of
shredded broccoli, carrots, and red cabbage)

2 bunches green onions (Slice whites and greens.)

3 cups slivered or sliced almonds

1 can of real bacon bits

3 cups cherry tomatoes, halved or quartered if they're
large

6 boneless, skinless chicken breasts, grilled or
sautéed in a small amount of vegetable oil

4 packages chicken or chicken teriyaki ramen
noodles

Dressing:

2/3 cup sugar

1 1/3 cup cider vinegar

2 cups oil

4 ramen noodle seasoning packages (see below)

*Salad can be assembled up to 1 hour before serving.
Combine the dressing ingredients and mix well. Divide
the coleslaw mixes and the green onions between two
large serving bowls. Divide the dressing between the
two serving bowls. Toss well. On top of the salads, layer
the cherry tomatoes, bacon bits, and almonds, dividing
the amounts between the two bowls. Chop the cooked
and cooled chicken breasts into very small pieces. Layer
the chicken on top of the almonds. Put the salads in the
refrigerator until time to serve.*

*When it's time to serve, place the salads on the table. Put
the dry ramen noodle blocks on a plate next to
the salads.*

SERVING TIPS

*It's very important not to add the
ramen noodles to this salad before
the Get-Together. The participants
will break the noodles into the bowl
and toss the salad to help them
discover important truths about our
"brokenness" before God.*

Rolls and Butter

*Serve with your favorite store-bought
rolls and butter.*

Cookies

*Serve your favorite homemade or
store-bought cookies.*

GET-TOGETHER 7

Trust your true self to Jesus and others.

FOOD CONNECTION

Today's Get-Together is about being transparent before Jesus and others. It's about trusting others enough to reveal our hidden selves. In each of today's options, there's something hidden that the participants will reveal when they dig in to the food.

Don't forget the paper goods!

Bring:

☐ plates

☐ bowls

☐ cups

☐ flatware

☐ napkins

as needed.

■ Quick and Easy MENU

- filled doughnuts
- beverages

Serve a variety of doughnuts with fruit, cream, and custard fillings.

■ Easy Plus MENU

- hidden snacks
- beverages

Purchase a variety of snacks such as cookies, candies, popcorn, chips, or snack mix—whatever your group likes. Portion out the snacks, putting each serving into a small plastic snack bag. Put each plastic snack bag into a paper lunch bag. Fold over the tops and either staple them shut or tie them with ribbon so that the participants won't be able to see the snacks inside. Mix up all the bags—there shouldn't be anything on the bags indicating what's inside them.

It's important that there are several different snacks and no one knows which snack he or she chose until the bag is opened.

■ High Impact MENU

- bean and rice burritos
- chicken fajita burritos
- beef and bean burritos
- burrito toppings
- beverages
- vanilla ice cream with cinnamon *dulce de leche* sauce

Bean and Rice Burritos *(makes about 8)*

1 can Spanish rice (or one box, prepared according to the package directions)
1 can refried beans
2 cups shredded cheese
8 large flour tortillas

Set the oven to 325° F. Warm the Spanish rice, the beans, and the tortillas. Layer 1/4 cup beans, 1/4 cup rice, and 1/4 cup cheese in the middle of a tortilla. Fold the bottom edge of the tortilla over the filling. Fold the sides over the filling. Roll up the tortilla and secure with a toothpick. Place on a baking sheet in the oven until hot—about 20 to 30 minutes. Serve with burrito toppings.

Chicken Fajita Burritos *(makes about 8)*

2 pounds boneless, skinless chicken breasts
1 large sweet onion
1 large green pepper
1 large red pepper
Italian dressing
8 large flour tortillas

Slice the chicken breasts, peppers, and onion into thin slices. Sauté in a small amount of Italian dressing until cooked through. Warm the tortillas in the microwave. Place 1/8 of the meat and vegetables on a tortilla. Fold the bottom edge of the tortilla over the filling. Fold the sides over the filling. Roll up the tortilla and secure with a toothpick. Place on a baking sheet in the oven until hot—about 20 to 30 minutes. Serve with burrito toppings.

Beef Burritos *(makes about 8)*

2 pounds hamburger
2 packages taco seasoning
1 can tomatoes and green chilis
1 can pinto beans
8 large flour tortillas

Brown the hamburger, and drain the grease. Prepare taco meat according to the directions on the taco-seasoning packet. Stir in one can of tomatoes and green chilis. Drain the pinto beans, and stir them into the mixture. Warm the tortillas. Place 1/8 of the meat on a tortilla. Fold the bottom edge of the tortilla over the filling. Fold the sides over the filling. Roll up the tortilla and secure with a toothpick. Place on a baking sheet in the oven until hot—about 20 to 30 minutes. Serve with burrito toppings.

Burrito Toppings
shredded lettuce
shredded cheese
salsa
chopped tomatoes
chopped green onions
sour cream
canned green chili, warmed

SERVING TIPS

Plan on at least two burritos per person. Part of the fun for this meal is that people won't know what's inside the burritos, so you can mix them up, put them all on one baking sheet, and serve them all on one platter.

An easier option for this meal would be to purchase frozen burritos with various fillings or to only make two of the varieties listed here.

Vanilla Ice Cream With Cinnamon *Dulce de Leche* Sauce

Serve vanilla ice cream with this luscious sauce. Combine 1 cup whipping cream with 1 packed cup of dark brown sugar and 1/2 teaspoon cinnamon. Gently boil until the mixture is reduced to 1 cup. Stir in 1/2 cup sweetened condensed milk. The sauce can be made ahead, but it should be warmed before serving.

Experience forgiveness through Jesus and others.

FOOD CONNECTION

In today's Get-Together, participants will talk about how forgiveness softens us. All of today's food options feature food that is softened before it's eaten.

Don't forget the paper goods!

Bring:

- ☐ plates
- ☐ bowls
- ☐ cups
- ☐ flatware
- ☐ napkins

as needed.

■ Quick and Easy MENU

- biscotti
- beverages

Purchase biscotti. Serve with hot chocolate or coffee to dip the biscotti in.

■ Easy Plus MENU

- beverages
- baked brie

Baked Brie   *(serves 8)*

One 1-pound round of Brie
1/3 cup brown sugar
2 tablespoons butter
1/2 cup chopped pecans

Preheat the oven to 325° F. Melt the butter and sauté the pecans in the butter until toasted. Put the brie on a baking sheet. Sprinkle the brown sugar on top. Then pour the butter and pecans over the top. Bake for 15 minutes until the brie is melted and the sugar begins to caramelize.

Serve with fancy crackers, sliced apples, and sliced pears.

■ High Impact MENU

- build-your-own french onion soup
- green salad
- beverages
- cookies

Build-Your-Own French Onion Soup

(serves 8 to 12 people)

1 stick of butter (don't substitute margarine)
8 cups onions, very thinly sliced
4 tablespoons flour
1 teaspoon pepper
1 teaspoon sugar
1 teaspoon Worcestershire sauce
3 quarts beef broth

Melt the butter over medium heat in a large heavy pan. Sauté the onions in the butter for up to an hour. They'll caramelize and sweeten the longer they cook. Sprinkle the flour, pepper, and sugar on the onions. Add the Worcestershire sauce and the beef broth. Bring to a boil. Then lower heat and simmer for at least 20 minutes to blend the flavors.

Meanwhile, slice a loaf of french bread and toast in a 325-degree oven until well toasted on both sides.

SERVING TIPS

Leave the soup in the cooking pot on the stove. Place swiss cheese slices and the toasted bread on a platter next to the soup, along with oven-proof bowls. Heat the oven to 425° F. Put slips of paper, a pen, and a large baking sheet nearby.

Have each person write his or her name on a slip of paper. Have everyone fill a bowl with soup, place a piece of toast on top of the soup, and lay a slice of cheese on top of the bread. Have people put their bowls of soup on the baking sheet and slip their name underneath. Put the soup bowls in the oven.

Invite everyone to begin on a salad while the soup cooks. Cook the soup until the cheese is melted and bubbly. Then serve each person his or her own bowl of soup. Be sure to use care, the bowls will be very hot.

Green Salad

1 head romaine lettuce, washed and torn in small pieces
1 package prewashed baby spinach
4 green onions, chopped whites and greens
2/3 cup roasted sunflower seeds
1 or 2 ripe avocados, chopped
1 to 2 cups broccoli or radish sprouts, well washed

Mix all the ingredients in a large bowl. Toss with just enough of the dressing to barely coat all the ingredients.

Dressing

2 hard-boiled eggs, mashed while still warm
1/2 teaspoon salt
2 teaspoons sugar
3/4 tablespoon freshly ground pepper
1 clove garlic, crushed
1/2 cup salad oil
1 1/2 tablespoons Dijon mustard
6 tablespoons heavy cream
1/2 cup red wine vinegar

Place mashed eggs in a blender. One at a time and in order, add each ingredient to the blender. Blend after each addition. When all ingredients have been added, blend until smooth and emulsified.

SERVING TIPS

Prepare the salad, and then toss with the dressing just as people are arriving. Place the salad on the table while people are preparing their french onion soup. Provide salad plates. Invite people to help themselves to the salad and to chat while they're waiting for their soup to cook.

Cookies

End today's meal with your favorite cookies.

GET-TOGETHER
9

*Value the
little things
with Jesus
and others.*

FOOD CONNECTION

Today's Get-Together is about valuing the little things in our friendships with Jesus and others. All of today's food options include little tidbits of food.

*Don't forget the
paper goods!*

Bring:

☐ plates
☐ bowls
☐ cups
☐ flatware
☐ napkins

as needed.

■ Quick and Easy MENU

- mini-snacks

Purchase mini-snacks such as Ritz Bits Sandwiches, with cheese or peanut butter, or mini Chips Ahoy! cookies. If you're meeting in the morning, purchase mini-doughnuts.

■ Easy Plus MENU

- assorted cheese cubes

Purchase bags of various kinds of cheese cubes. Pour the cubes out on a serving tray, and serve with toothpicks. If your grocery store doesn't carry cheese cubes, purchase a variety of cheese blocks and cut them into small cubes.

■ High Impact MENU

- mini-meatballs
- mini-sausages
- fresh fruit tray
- assorted cheese cubes
- fresh veggie tray
- mini-cheesecakes

Mini-Meatballs

1 large package frozen meatballs
2 packages brown gravy mix

Fill a slow cooker with frozen meatballs. Mix the gravy mix according to the package directions. Pour over the meatballs. Heat on low for 4 to 5 hours.

Fresh Fruit Tray

Cut up fresh fruit, and arrange it attractively on a platter. Serve with toothpicks.

Mini-Sausages

2 pound package of little
   smokies sausages
1 large jar grape jelly
1 large jar chili sauce

Mix the grape jelly and chili sauce in a large saucepan. Add the little smokies sausages and simmer 30 minutes.

Fresh Veggie Tray

Cut up fresh veggies, and arrange them attractively on a platter. Serve with ranch dressing.

Mini-Cheesecakes

One 8-ounce package cream
   cheese, softened
1/2 cup sugar
2 cups thawed Cool Whip
12 vanilla wafers
assorted candies such as
   mini chocolate chips,
   toffee chips, or sprinkles
paper cupcake liners

Beat the cream cheese and sugar. Gently fold in the Cool Whip. Place cupcake liners in a muffin pan. Place a vanilla wafer in the bottom of each liner. Spoon the cheese mixture on top of each vanilla wafer. Sprinkle the top of each mini-cheesecake with candy. Refrigerate for several hours before serving.

Assorted Cheese Cubes

Purchase bags of various kinds of cheese cubes. Pour the cubes out on a serving tray and serve with toothpicks. If your grocery store doesn't carry cheese cubes, purchase a variety of cheese blocks, and cut them into small cubes.

GET-TOGETHER 10

Work through the tough stuff with Jesus and others.

FOOD CONNECTION

All of the food options today can be messy to eat. Relationships can be messy too! Today's food options will help participants talk about how to handle the messy stuff that comes up in relationships all the time.

Don't forget the paper goods!

Bring:

- ☐ plates
- ☐ bowls
- ☐ cups
- ☐ flatware
- ☐ napkins

as needed.

■ Quick and Easy MENU

- powdered-sugar doughnuts

Purchase powdered-sugar doughnuts from a grocery store or bakery.

■ Easy Plus MENU

- s'mores

Purchase graham crackers, milk chocolate bars, and marshmallows. Provide one candle in a candleholder for every two or three people. Votive candles or tapers both work for this snack.

Place the candles on a table at which the participants will be seated. Light the candles. Have everyone toast their marshmallows on metal forks or metal shish-ke-bab skewers over the candles. Have the participants scrape the toasted marshmallows onto a graham cracker topped with half of a chocolate bar. Top the marshmallow with another graham cracker.

■ High Impact MENU

- Cajun boil
- rolls and butter
- beverages
- caramel brownies

Cajun Boil

1/2 pound kielbasa per person
1/2 pound large, raw shrimp in
   the shell per person
2 to 3 small red potatoes per person
1 ear of corn per person
1 small onion per person
1 lemon for every two people
3/4 cup Old Bay Seasoning
1 pound butter
cocktail sauce
Dijon mustard

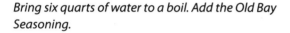

Bring six quarts of water to a boil. Add the Old Bay Seasoning.

Cut the sausage into 2-inch pieces. Wash the potatoes, and cut them in half. Clean the corn, and break the cobs in half. Peel the onions, and cut them in quarters. Scrub the lemons, and cut them in quarters. Half an hour before everyone will arrive, put the sausage, corn, potatoes, onions, and lemons in the water, and boil for 20 minutes. While everything's boiling, put cocktail sauce and mustard into small bowls. Melt the butter, and pour it into several small bowls. When the potatoes are tender, rinse the shrimp, and add them to the pot. Gently stir. Turn off the heat.

SERVING TIPS

Cover the table with one or two layers of butcher paper or paper tablecloths. Keep all the food in the kitchen until everyone has arrived and is seated at the table. After the meal has been prayed for, quickly drain the liquid from the pot. Careful! The steam can burn quickly! Return the food to the pot, and take the pot to the dining table. Have all the participants lift up the edges of the tablecloth. Dump out the food in the middle of the table. Bring out the condiments, a basket of rolls, and serve beverages. No utensils are allowed! People eat with their hands, so provide lots of napkins—you may even want to provide wet washcloths at the end of the meal.

Caramel Brownies

Make your favorite brownies in a 9x13-inch pan. While the brownies are baking, melt 20 caramel candies with 3 tablespoons of milk. Immediately after taking the brownies from the oven, sprinkle 2/3 cup chocolate chips over the top. Drizzle with the caramel. Cool completely before cutting.

Stick with Jesus and others.

FOOD CONNECTION

All of today's food is sticky to help participants understand the importance of sticking with Jesus and others.

Don't forget the paper goods!

Bring:

- ☐ plates
- ☐ bowls
- ☐ cups
- ☐ flatware
- ☐ napkins

as needed.

■ Quick and Easy MENU

- cinnamon rolls
- beverages

Purchase gooey cinnamon rolls from your local grocery store or bakery.

■ Easy Plus MENU

- beverages
- orange sticky buns

Orange Sticky Buns   *(serves 6 to 8)*

2 cups flour
3 teaspoons baking powder
1 teaspoon salt
1/3 cup vegetable oil
2/3 cup milk

1/4 cup pancake syrup
8 tablespoons melted butter, divided
1/3 cup frozen orange juice concentrate
3/4 cup brown sugar, packed
1 teaspoon cinnamon

Preheat oven to 375° F. Stir together the flour, baking powder, and salt. Add oil and milk, and stir until mixture forms a ball. Set aside. Spray an 8-inch cake pan with baking spray. Mix pancake syrup and 4 tablespoons melted butter. Spread into the pan so it covers the entire bottom of the pan. Mix together the remaining butter and orange juice concentrate in a small bowl. Mix the brown sugar and cinnamon on a dinner plate. Pat out the biscuit dough on a floured surface until it's half an inch thick. Cut rounds with a small glass or biscuit cutter. Dip the biscuit into the butter and orange juice mixture. Then dip into the sugar mixture. Place in cake pan. Continue until all the dough has been placed in the pan. Bake for about 30 minutes. Cool in pan for 10 minutes. Turn onto a plate. Serve warm.

■ High Impact MENU

- maple-glazed chicken
- rice pilaf
- green salad
- cookies

Maple-Glazed Chicken

1 chicken leg per person
1 chicken thigh per person
2 slices bacon per person
3/4 cup maple syrup
3/4 cup ketchup
1/2 cup apricot preserves
1/2 teaspoon ground cloves
1 tablespoon Worcestershire sauce
3 cloves garlic, crushed
1 tablespoon lemon juice

Wrap each chicken piece with a slice of bacon, secure the bacon with a toothpick, and place the chicken in a baking pan. Mix together the maple syrup, ketchup, apricot preserves, cloves, Worcestershire sauce, garlic, and lemon juice in a small saucepan and heat until well combined. Brush each chicken piece with the sauce and bake at 400° F for about 45 minutes or until done.

Rice Pilaf   *(serves 8)*

1/4 cup butter
1 small onion, finely chopped
1 1/2 cup rice
3 cups chicken broth
1/4 teaspoon pepper
1 cup frozen peas
1/2 cup slivered almonds

Sauté the onion in the butter. Add the rice, and stir until the rice is golden. Add the broth. Cook 20 to 30 minutes until the rice is tender. Stir in the peas and almonds. Cook until the peas are hot.

An easier option would be to add peas and almonds to a boxed rice pilaf mix.

Green Salad
Serve your favorite green salad with this meal.

Cookies
Serve this meal with your favorite store-bought or homemade cookies.

GET-TOGETHER 13

Live friendship first with Jesus and others.

FOOD CONNECTION

In today's Get-Together, participants will explore the fruitfulness of friendship. All of today's food has a fruit theme.

Don't forget the paper goods!

Bring:

- ☐ plates
- ☐ bowls
- ☐ cups
- ☐ flatware
- ☐ napkins

as needed.

■ Quick and Easy MENU

- fresh fruit trays

Purchase already prepared fresh fruit trays from your grocery store's deli. Or provide a variety of fresh fruit such as grapes, strawberries, and bananas.

■ Easy Plus MENU

- fruit smoothies

Set out vanilla yogurt, bananas, and a variety of fruit juices. Also set out frozen strawberries, blueberries, peaches, and raspberries. Provide one blender for every three to four people. Invite everyone to make a fruit smoothie by blending his or her choice of juice, yogurt, and fruit together.

■ High Impact MENU

- grilled chicken and pineapple sandwiches
- fruit salad
- mini fruit "pizzas"

Grilled Chicken and Pineapple Sandwiches

1 skinless, boneless chicken breast for each person
1 pineapple ring per person
1/2 cup teriyaki sauce
1 tablespoon honey
1 teaspoon grated ginger root
sandwich rolls
honey mustard dressing

Mix the teriyaki sauce, honey, and ginger root. Heat a grill. Brush chicken breasts with the teriyaki mixture and grill until cooked through. The last few minutes of cooking, brush the pineapple slices with the teriyaki sauce, and grill until heated through. Watch carefully— the pineapple will burn quickly.

Top each chicken breast with a pineapple slice. Serve on sandwich rolls with honey mustard dressing.

Mini Fruit Pizzas

1 tube of sugar cookie dough
8-ounce package of cream cheese, softened
1/3 cup powdered sugar
1/2 teaspoon vanilla extract
1/2 cup apricot preserves
1 tablespoon water
fruit (sliced strawberries, fresh blueberries, banana slices, kiwi slices, and mandarin orange sections)

Bake the sugar cookies according to the package directions. Combine the cream cheese, powdered sugar, and vanilla extract. When the cookies are cool, spread each cookie with the frosting. Arrange the fruit on top. Heat the apricot preserves and water in the microwave. Brush the glaze over the fruit. Refrigerate until ready to serve.

An easier option would be to serve frozen fruit and juice bars.

Fruit Salad
Make a large fruit salad with in-season fruit. Check your grocery store's deli. They may already have a fruit salad you can purchase.